Guinea

WORLD BIBLIOGRAPHICAL SERIES

General Editors:
Robert G. Neville (Executive Editor)
John J. Horton

Robert A. Myers   Hans H. Wellisch
Ian Wallace   Ralph Lee Woodward, Jr.

John J. Horton is Deputy Librarian of the University of Bradford and was formerly Chairman of its Academic Board of Studies in Social Sciences. He has maintained a longstanding interest in the discipline of area studies and its associated bibliographical problems, with special reference to European Studies. In particular he has published in the field of Icelandic and of Yugoslav studies, including the two relevant volumes in the World Bibliographical Series.

Robert A. Myers is Associate Professor of Anthropology in the Division of Social Sciences and Director of Study Abroad Programs at Alfred University, Alfred, New York. He has studied post-colonial island nations of the Caribbean and has spent two years in Nigeria on a Fulbright Lectureship. His interests include international public health, historical anthropology and developing societies. In addition to *Amerindians of the Lesser Antilles: a bibliography* (1981), *A Resource Guide to Dominica, 1493-1986* (1987) and numerous articles, he has compiled the World Bibliographical Series volumes on *Dominica* (1987), *Nigeria* (1989) and *Ghana* (1991).

Ian Wallace is Professor of German at the University of Bath. A graduate of Oxford in French and German, he also studied in Tübingen, Heidelberg and Lausanne before taking teaching posts at universities in the USA, Scotland and England. He specializes in contemporary German affairs, especially literature and culture, on which he has published numerous articles and books. In 1979 he founded the journal *GDR Monitor*, which he continues to edit under its new title *German Monitor*.

Hans H. Wellisch is Professor emeritus at the College of Library and Information Services, University of Maryland. He was President of the American Society of Indexers and was a member of the International Federation for Documentation. He is the author of numerous articles and several books on indexing and abstracting, and has published *The Conversion of Scripts and Indexing and Abstracting: an International Bibliography*, and *Indexing from A to Z*. He also contributes frequently to *Journal of the American Society for Information Science*, *The Indexer* and other professional journals.

Ralph Lee Woodward, Jr. is Professor of History at Tulane University, New Orleans. He is the author of *Central America, a Nation Divided*, 2nd ed. (1985), as well as several monographs and more than seventy scholarly articles on modern Latin America. He has also compiled volumes in the World Bibliographical Series on *Belize* (1980), *El Salvador* (1988), *Guatemala* (Rev. Ed.) (1992) and *Nicaragua* (Rev. Ed.) (1994). Dr. Woodward edited the Central American section of the *Research Guide to Central America and the Caribbean* (1985) and is currently associate editor of Scribner's *Encyclopedia of Latin American History*.

VOLUME 191

Guinea

Margaret Binns

Compiler

CLIO PRESS

OXFORD, ENGLAND · SANTA BARBARA, CALIFORNIA
DENVER, COLORADO

British Library Cataloguing in Publication Data

Binns, Margaret
Guinea. – (World bibliographical series; vol. 191)
1. Guinea – Bibliography
I. Title
016.9′6652

ISBN 1–85109–148–3

ABC-CLIO Ltd.,
Old Clarendon Ironworks,
35A Great Clarendon Street,
Oxford OX2 6AT, England.

———

ABC-CLIO Inc.,
130 Cremona Drive,
Santa Barbara,
CA 93116, USA.

Designed by Bernard Crossland.
Typeset by Columns Design and Production Services Ltd., Reading, England.
Printed and bound in Great Britain by Bookcraft (Bath) Ltd., Midsomer Norton.

THE WORLD BIBLIOGRAPHICAL SERIES

This series, which is principally designed for the English speaker, will eventually cover every country (and many of the world's principal regions), each in a separate volume comprising annotated entries on works dealing with its history, geography, economy and politics; and with its people, their culture, customs, religion and social organization. Attention will also be paid to current living conditions – housing, education, newspapers, clothing, etc.– that are all too often ignored in standard bibliographies; and to those particular aspects relevant to individual countries. Each volume seeks to achieve, by use of careful selectivity and critical assessment of the literature, an expression of the country and an appreciation of its nature and national aspirations, to guide the reader towards an understanding of its importance. The keynote of the series is to provide, in a uniform format, an interpretation of each country that will express its culture, its place in the world, and the qualities and background that make it unique. The views expressed in individual volumes, however, are not necessarily those of the publisher.

VOLUMES IN THE SERIES

*To my parents for allowing me
to take them for granted.*

Contents

Contents

Contents

Preface

The major problem encountered when compiling this bibliography was the lack of published material, especially recent works, relating to Guinea. Volumes in the *World Bibliographical Series* are intended to be selective and to include publications from all subject areas, in order to provide a balanced overview of the country. However, this proved to be difficult and in some subject areas, such as history, I had to be more selective in the interests of balance, than in other areas where I had trouble identifying any publications at all. There is very little writing on Guinea in English and consequently, about half the items included are in French.

The vast majority of works on Guinea are by, or about, Ahmed Sekou Touré, the President, who, as leader of the Parti démocratique de Guinée (PDG) (Democratic Party of Guinea), led the country to independence in 1958 and maintained power until his death in 1984. Sekou Touré himself produced huge quantities of publications, largely propaganda material promoting his political views and achievements. Indeed, during the first part of his presidency many other writers hailed him as a hero, who, with his socialist revolutionary policies, was turning the country around from the exploitation and domination of colonialism to a period of economic rebirth and equality. However, it soon became apparent, and this can be traced in the writings about him, that Sekou Touré was in fact a paranoid dictator who ruthlessly crushed any opposition. Indeed, the reason he remained in power for so long was that all political opponents fled the country, or were tortured or killed in several notorious prison camps. This period of Sekou Touré's régime has generated many publications, written at the time or more recently, and I had to be fairly selective about which to include, in order to avoid top-heaviness.

In contrast, writings about Guinea during the period under Lansana Conté since 1984, are noticeable by their absence. There is really very little recent material, which proved to be something of a problem when compiling this bibliography. I often had to toss up whether or not to include a rather marginal or specialist journal article, in the absence of anything more substantial.

Items included are monographs, periodical articles and chapters in edited books. Every item was examined in order to obtain accurate bibliographic information and each item is annotated to give an assessment of its content and value. Some items for which I obtained references from literature searches or from other publications could not be found for examination and are therefore not included. Therefore, for this reason and for the reasons of selectivity stated above, this does not claim to be a comprehensive bibliography. It is rather intended to be a useful research tool to guide users to the most relevant and easily obtainable items on particular subjects relating to Guinea.

The libraries where most of the research was undertaken, and where the majority of items are to be found, were the School of Oriental and African Studies, University of London; the Institute of Development Studies, Sussex; the University of Sussex; and Birmingham University. Libraries in France would no doubt have yielded more French material, but as the object of the bibliography was to include English material if possible, this hardly seemed necessary. There are no commercial publishers in Guinea itself and the Bibliothèque Nationale is apparently in a neglected condition, so it was not worthwhile actually visiting Guinea for the purposes of compiling the bibliography. However, I did speak to several people who have visited Guinea recently in order to build up some idea of conditions in the country.

The items are divided under subject headings in line with the *World Bibliographical Series* standard layout, and within the subject sections they are arranged alphabetically by author, or by title if there is no author. Cross-references are included at the end of each section to guide users to relevant items in different sections. The index includes authors, titles and subjects. The titles are in italics and only include the titles of actual publications, not periodical articles or book chapters, although in the latter case the title of the book itself is included.

Acknowledgements

I wish to thank the staff of all the libraries mentioned above, and especially those at the Institute of Development Studies for their continuing friendship and for allowing me to rummage in the restricted stacks. I also wish to thank Melissa Leach and James Fairhead for allowing me access to their personal collection of materials on Guinea, and to Reg Cline-Cole for his help at Birmingham University. Thanks also to Hazel Lintott for drawing the map. Finally, I must thank my husband, Tony, for his encouragement and for occasionally holding the domestic fort in order that I could visit London and Birmingham.

Margaret Binns
Sussex
April 1996

Introduction

The Republic of Guinea is one of the least-known countries in Africa. Its official name is République de Guinée, and it is also known as Guinée française (French Guinea) or Guinea-Conakry in order to distinguish the country from other Guineas. From the end of the 19th century Guinea was a French colony, but after severing its links with France and becoming independent in 1958 it shut itself off from the world, and is only recently beginning to re-emerge. Compared with other African countries Guinea has been remarkably stable politically, having had only two leaders since independence. However, its economy has been less successful, and it has failed to reap the benefits of its abundant natural resources.

Geography

With an area of 246,000 sq. km (95,000 sq. miles) Guinea is approximately the same size as the United Kingdom. It is situated on the West African coast, sharing borders with Guinea-Bissau, Senegal, Mali, Côte d'Ivoire, Liberia and Sierra Leone.

Until 1994 Guinea was divided into four administrative divisions, which themselves coincided with the four main geographical areas. Guinée maritime (Maritime Guinea) covered the coastal area, a region of shallow river estuaries covered by mangrove swamps, backed by a coastal plain and enriched by alluvium from the inland upland region. This is the region in which the main bauxite reserves of the country are found, especially in the Fria and Boké areas. The capital, Conakry, is situated on the coast where older hard rocks reach the sea, and bauxite is also found offshore on the Iles de Los. Moyenne Guinée (Middle Guinea) covered the Fouta Djallon, an area in the west-centre of Guinea composed of ancient sandstones, much of it over 900 m high, and forming a plateau with deeply incised and fertile river valleys, providing great hydroelectric potential. Haute Guinée (Upper Guinea) covered the area which stretches from the Fouta Djallon in the west to the Mali border in the east, an area of savanna, through which flow the upper reaches of the River Niger. Guinée forestière (Forested Guinea) was the mountainous region in the south of the country on the borders with Liberia and Côte d'Ivoire, an inaccessible area, but with substantial mineral deposits of iron ore, gold and diamonds. These four administrative divisions were reorganized in 1994 into seven regions: the coastal region split into Kindia and Boké, the Fouta Djallon split into Labé and Mamou, and the rest of the country divided into Faranah, Kankan and N'Zérékoré regions.

Guinea's climate varies throughout the different areas (see item no. 13). The coastal region has a monsoon climate with high temperatures throughout the year and heavy rainfall during the period from May to October, but virtually no rain during the rest of the year. Conakry has an average annual rainfall of 430 cm, of which 130 cm falls during July, making the highest monthly rainfall figure for West Africa. The Fouta Djallon has a more pleasant tropical climate, with the altitude giving lower temperatures and rainfall which is more evenly distributed throughout the year (see item no. 12). In the southern highland area the rainfall is higher again, but is more evenly distributed, with only one or two drier months.

History

The early history of Guinea, before the present boundaries were set, was a complicated pattern of movements of peoples from different parts of Africa, who brought a range of languages, religions and traditions. The empire of Ghana had influence over the northern Guinea area by the 9th century, and brought an influx of Malinké and Soussou people, who pushed the Baga, Coniagui and other original inhabitants towards the forest and coastal areas.

By the 13th century the Malinké had founded the great Mali empire, which stretched from the Atlantic to northern Nigeria. Its leader, Sundiata Keita (c.1205–55), established his capital at Niani, which is currently a small village in Upper Guinea, on the Sankaran river southeast of Siguiri.

From the 13th century onwards Muslim Fula immigrants began arriving from the north, in search of grazing for their cattle. By the 15th century they had become sufficiently settled in the Fouta Djallon for their leader, Koli Tengela, to declare independence from the Mali empire. More fervent Muslim Fulas moved into the area, and by the 18th century the Muslim Kingdom of Fouta Djallon (see item no. 111) was established under the leadership of Karamoko Alfa Bari. Its capital, Timbo, is now a village north-east of Mamou, where the remains of the 18th-century mosque can still be seen (see item nos. 25 and 27).

A rival centre was set up at Labé, which became a centre of Islamic teaching. Alfa Yaya (or Alfa Labé), the great-grandson of Alfa Bari, became leader of a state as powerful as that based at Timbo (see item no. 86). Today, he is hailed as a hero for his resistance to the French colonial advances at the end of the 19th century, and his tomb can still be seen in Labé.

Colonial period

Portuguese, British, and later French merchants had been active on the coast from the 15th century, and Conakry, then known as Tumbo, was a port used in the slave trade (see item nos. 35 and 40). But, as the 'Scramble for Africa' accelerated during the 19th century the French gained control over the Rivières du Sud (Rivers of the South), as the coastal area was known. France acquired rights over Conakry in 1880, and the borders of modern Guinea were fixed soon afterwards. In 1893 Guinea became an autonomous colony under French rule.

However, the French experienced great resistance from the interior of the country, especially from the Fouta Djallon. The Malinké chief, Samori Touré, proved to be a thorn in the flesh for the French, and with his guerrilla army he managed to hold off the French advance until his capture and deportation to Gabon in 1898 (see item no. 42).

For the next sixty years Guinea was a French colony, although the traditional chiefs continued to exercise administrative control. The French exploited Guinea's resources to the full. Wild rubber was the principal export before the First World War, and supported a community of Lebanese intermediaries in Conakry. The French later developed cash-crop plantations, growing coffee, bananas, groundnuts and palm oil, and began the exploitation of Guinea's rich bauxite reserves, as well as exporting gold, diamonds and iron ore.

Between 1902 and 1914 the French built a railway from Conakry to Kankan, for strategic reasons as much as for trade (see item no. 53). Kankan, situated on the Milo River in eastern Guinea, and linked by river with Mali, was the centre of a Muslim trading empire in the 19th century. The railway still runs sporadically today.

Independence

After the Second World War the first moves were made towards Guinean independence. At a conference in Mali in 1946, a group of African politicians formed the Rassemblement démocratique africaine

(RDA) (African Democratic Rally) (see item no. 133). One of the delegates to this conference was Ahmed Sekou Touré, a Malinké who claimed Samori Touré as an ancestor. He had already founded Guinea's first trade union, that of the Post and Telecommunications Workers, and in 1947 he and others founded the Parti démocratique de Guinée (PDG) (Democratic Party of Guinea) as an affiliate of the RDA.

Although failing to win membership of the French Assembly in 1954 (in an election widely thought to have been rigged by the French), Sekou Touré was elected mayor of Conakry in 1955, and was finally elected to the French Assembly in 1956. In the territorial elections of 1957 the PDG won fifty-seven of the sixty seats and Sekou Touré effectively became prime minister.

One of his first acts was the abolition of chieftaincy (see item no. 80), in order to bring the whole country under the authority of the PDG. This caused resentment, particularly among the Fula of the Fouta Djallon, where the chieftaincy system had still been very strong. This was the beginning of the tensions between the Fula and the Malinké, who held the reigns of power.

When, in 1958, the French under General de Gaulle offered Guinea the opportunity to join a community of French African states, Sekou Touré was strongly opposed to the proposal. Consequently, in a referendum on 28th September 1958, ninety-five per cent of Guineans voted against joining the French community (see item no. 51). On 2nd October, independence was declared. Following Guinea's overwhelming rejection of their government, the French abruptly withdrew all support and investment from the country. Sekou Touré had declared that the people of Guinea would 'prefer poverty in freedom to riches in slavery', and was more than happy to see them go.

Sekou Touré's government (1958–84)

Sekou Touré began his presidency surrounded by great popular support and a general mood of optimism for his revolutionary socialist policies. Following France's withdrawal Guinea was left in an economic vacuum, but Sekou Touré obtained aid from the Soviet Union and other Eastern-bloc countries, causing the United States to worry about the spread of communism in Africa (see item no. 135). However, Sekou Touré's policies were more anti-capitalist than pro-communist and relations with the Soviet Union soon deteriorated. The Soviet ambassador was expelled in 1961 following accusations of involvement in the 'Teachers' plot', a supposed attempt to encourage left-wing student ideas.

Sekou Touré maintained his hold on power by the encouragement of nepotism in the Malinké clan of which he was the central figure. Huge sums of money and diamonds were hoarded abroad, while the Guinean people endured shortages and hardship. Anyone suspected of political opposition, especially the Fula, would 'disappear' or be sent to one of the prison camps, of which Boiro was the most notorious (see item nos. 62 and 66). Throughout his presidency Sekou Touré was convinced that his political opponents were plotting against him, and he became increasingly paranoid and ruthless in the eradication of his supposed enemies. Many educated Guineans fled to exile in neighbouring countries, which had the effect of further weakening the economic situation. By the mid-1960s Guinea had entered a period of isolationism and internal oppression. In an attempt to control both internal and external trade, there was a widespread crackdown on market traders in November 1964 and severe punishments for anyone caught smuggling or illegally dealing with foreign currencies. Guinea had withdrawn from the Communauté financière Africaine (CFA) Franc Zone in 1960 and the Guinea franc had become virtually worthless outside the country.

In 1965, opposition exiles in Côte d'Ivoire and Senegal, with support from Paris, formed the Front pour la libération de Guinée (FLING) (Guinea Liberation Front). Following the 'Traders' plot' in 1966, a failed attempt to install a more liberal government backed by FLING, relations with France were completely severed.

On the night of 21st/22nd November 1970 an attempted invasion took place from the sea off Conakry. Some 350 Portuguese-led troops attacked many public buildings and freed a number of political prisoners. However, although Sekou Touré claimed that he had defeated an attempted coup, the real target of the troops was the headquarters of the Partido Africano da Independência da Guiné e Cabo Verde (PAIGC) (African Party for the Independence of Guinea and Cape Verde), a group fighting for the independence of Guinea-Bissau from Portugal (see item nos. 70 and 84).

Nevertheless, there were severe reprisals, as Sekou Touré took the opportunity to weaken any opposition. At least ninety people were executed and many others were imprisoned and tortured, including several former ministers and the archbishop of Conakry. In 1973 the leader of the PAIGC, Amílcar Cabral, was assassinated in Conakry, leading to further suspicions of plots against Sekou Touré.

Accordingly, Sekou Touré's paranoia grew at this time and he sought to tighten his control of the country. One of the measures he took was to expand the powers of the Pouvoirs révolutionnaires locaux (PRLs) (Local Revolutionary Power), which had been set up in 1968 as local revolutionary authorities to maintain control at village level. In 1973 local government structures were reorganized, and the PRLs were given more authority to control all trading activities, which made them, in effect, the 'economic police'. The Fula in the Fouta Djallon became the focus of Sekou Touré's paranoia, with the announcement in 1976 of the discovery of a 'Fula plot', and the declaration that the Fula were the 'enemies of socialism'. Diallo Telli, the minister of justice and first secretary-general of the Organisation of African Unity, was accused of leading the plot, which was allegedly backed by the US Central Intelligence Agency. He was arrested and died of starvation in Boiro prison camp in 1977 (see item nos. 66 and 89). It was estimated that in six months of 1974 over 250 people were executed in Camp Boiro alone. Many thousands of Guineans, particularly Fula, continued to flee the country.

By 1976 Guinea was economically paralysed. All private trade had been banned in 1975, the borders were closed and smugglers were shot. The 'economic police' were themselves widely suspected of smuggling and corruption. Diplomatic relations with France were patched up in 1976 and an economic agreement was reached that included the banning of Guinean dissident propaganda in Paris.

In August 1977 there was a spontaneous uprising and rioting by market women across the country, who, due to the crippling trading restrictions, could no longer afford to buy their own produce. This began a reversal in economic policy, with Sekou Touré disbanding the 'economic police' and allowing the resumption of some private trade. In response to a damning report in 1978 by Amnesty International on the human rights situation in Guinea (see item no. 59), and criticisms from the international community, a process of liberalization was begun. From January 1979 the country was renamed the People's Revolutionary Republic of Guinea.

During the early 1980s Sekou Touré cultivated the image of a Pan-Africanist and attempted to rebuild relations with neighbouring countries. But, on 26th March 1984 Sekou Touré died suddenly of a heart attack, leaving a power vacuum with no successor ready to take over.

Lansana Conté's government (1984-)

On 3rd April 1984, in a peaceful coup, Colonels Lansana Conté and Diarra Traoré, as leaders of the Comité militaire de redressement national (CMRN) (Military Committee for National Recovery), took over as president and prime minister respectively. The PDG and the old party structures were dismantled, political prisoners were released, and a semi-civilian government was appointed. In May, the country's name was changed back to the Republic of Guinea. This second republic was greeted with enthusiasm as the CMRN promised a new era of freedom and denounced Sekou Touré's 'bloody and pitiless dictatorship'.

However, Lansana Conté did not possess the eloquence or charisma of Sekou Touré and soon ran into opposition from his prime minister. In July 1985 Traoré and some fellow Malinké officers staged a coup while Conté was out of the country. This attempt was unsuccessful and Traoré and more than 200 others were arrested. Nearly two years later, in 1987, it was announced that Traoré and sixty others had been tried and were to be executed, although it was widely presumed that they had in fact been killed soon after their arrest.

Lansana Conté's swift response to the coup attempt strengthened his position, and the country was soon swarming with economic and technical advisors. Structural adjustment programmes were imposed by the World Bank and International Monetary Fund in return for economic funding (see item nos. 145, 146 and 151). However, the austerity measures associated with this economic restructuring, as well as the streamlining of the civil service and the reorganization of the judicial system, led to a certain amount of dissatisfaction and unrest, particularly among the Malinké who felt that the government was becoming dominated by the Soussou (Lansana Conté's ethnic group). Numerous cabinet reshuffles took place in an attempt to maintain control.

In October 1989 President Conté announced the timetable for the return to civilian rule under a two-party system. A new draft constitution (loi fondamentale) was submitted to a national referendum on 23rd December 1990 and received the support of 98.7 per cent of those who voted. This led to the disbanding of the military CMRN and its replacement by the Comité transitoire de redressement national (CTRN) (Transitional Committee for National Recovery) to oversee the transition period leading to elections for president and legislature.

In October 1991, in response to a certain amount of popular unrest, Conté announced that, contrary to earlier proposals, there would be unlimited registration of political parties. This came into effect with the constitution of the third republic on 23rd December 1991. The CTRN and the government were extensively reorganized in accordance with the new constitution, and a pro-Conté party, the Parti de l'unité et du progrès (PUP) (Party of Unity and Progress) was formed. Among the first parties to be registered in April 1992 was the Rassemblement populaire guinéen (RPG) (Rally of the Guinean People), which had been an illegal opposition group for some years, led by Alpha Condé. By the end of 1992 more than forty political parties had been officially recognized. All the parties had strong regional and ethnic support, leading to a number of clashes between supporters of rival parties.

Legislative elections were originally planned for 1992 with the presidential election in early 1993. But repeated delays and postponements meant that the presidential election was held in

December 1993, and the legislative elections were held in June 1995. General Conté beat seven other candidates in the presidential election, gaining 51.7 per cent of the votes cast. Alpha Condé gained 19.6 per cent of the votes to give him second place.

On 11th June 1995 elections were finally held for the new Assemblée nationale to replace the CTRN. The 114 seats comprised three seats for each of the thirty-eight constituencies. Twenty-one of the registered political parties presented a total of 846 candidates, while eleven parties combined into four opposition coalitions. The PUP won seventy-one seats, and the RPG won nineteen. Two other leading opposition parties, the Parti du renouveau et du progrès (PRP) (Party of Renewal and Progress) and the Union pour la nouvelle république (UNR) (Union for the New Republic), won nine seats each. The remaining six seats went to five other parties. Nine of the elected members were women.

There were widespread allegations of election-rigging from the opposition, who threatened to boycott the parliament, but foreign observers were happy that the elections had been conducted properly and fairly. On 30th August 1995 the inaugural session of the Assemblée nationale was held and elected Boubacar Biro Diallo as speaker. Rather than boycotting the legislature as threatened, twelve opposition parties joined forces as the Coordination de l'opposition démocratique (Codem) (Coordination of the Democratic Opposition), under the leadership of Ba Mamadou.

President Conté's position began to look increasingly insecure on 2nd February 1996 when up to 2,000 soldiers took to the streets of Conakry, initially to demand a salary increase; but, they stormed the presidential palace, large parts of which were destroyed, and captured General Conté. The president was taken to the army barracks, where he was forced to sign a document submitting to the soldiers' demands. Conté's position in power was only maintained by this agreement and by the arrival of loyalist troops. An estimated 50 people were killed and 100 wounded during this uprising.

Population and society

The latest census, taken in 1992, estimated the population at 5.6 million, including approximately 560,000 refugees from the conflicts in Liberia and Sierra Leone (see item no. 94). However, this is thought to be an underestimate and the true population is probably nearer 7.5 million, with a rapidly increasing number of refugees. Another census is planned for 1996. Before the mid-1980s, up to two million Guineans had themselves sought refuge abroad from the harsh dictatorship of Sekou Touré. Many of these have now returned.

The population is made up of a number of ethnic groups. The coastal region, which covers about sixteen per cent of the country, is home to about twenty per cent of the population, mostly Soussou (or Susu) and also Baga. The Soussou make up the dominant group in the present government. Conakry is home to about one million people. The Fouta Djallon supports about forty per cent of the population, mostly Fula (also known as Peul, Fulani, Fulbe), a large group of nomadic pastoralists who have spread across a wide area of West Africa. Despite being the largest ethnic group in the country, the Fula have always been under-represented in official circles. Haute Guinée has the lowest population density, with twenty-one per cent of the population, mostly Malinké (Mandingo, Mandinka) spread across forty per cent of the land. The remaining nineteen per cent of the population who live in Guinée forestière comprise a number of smaller ethnic groups including Kissi, Kono, Guerzé, and Toma.

Demographic indicators are among the worst in Africa. Life expectancy at birth is only forty-four for both men and women, and twenty-five per cent of children die before the age of five. Only thirteen per cent of the population have access to health care. However, the population is growing by approximately 2.8 per cent per year.

Education was disrupted during the Sekou Touré era when French was replaced by indigenous languages as the medium of instruction (see item no. 186). Since 1985 this policy has been overturned and steps are being taken to improve primary schooling (see item no. 187). However, literacy is estimated at only twenty-five per cent, with the vast majority of women being illiterate (see item no. 118). Of school-age children, only thirty-seven per cent attend primary school, and only ten per cent receive secondary education.

Islam is the principal religion, with about eighty-five per cent of the population holding Muslim beliefs. Only about five per cent are Christian, mainly in the Conakry area, while in the forested south-east of the country animist beliefs are still common.

Foreign relations

Relations with France have blown hot and cold over the years (see the 'History' section above). They are currently friendly, with France being one of Guinea's major trading partners. Guinea's period of isolationism under Sekou Touré meant that relations with some of its neighbours were strained for some time. However, in 1980 Guinea joined both the Gambia River Development Organisation (GRDO) with Senegal and The Gambia, and the Mano River Union with Sierra Leone and Liberia (see item no. 131). In recent years Guinea has attempted to mediate in the civil wars taking place in both Liberia and Sierra Leone, and has become the destination for many hundreds of thousands of refugees fleeing from these conflicts.

Economy

Despite an abundance of natural resources, which could enable Guinea to be one of the richest countries in Africa, it remains one of the poorest, with gross national product (GNP) per head at approximately $500. Sekou Touré's legacy of economic mismanagement has been difficult to overturn. Soon after taking power in 1984 Lansana Conté negotiated a structural adjustment agreement with the International Monetary Fund linked to a programme of economic and financial reform (PREF), designed to encourage economic recovery. This involved a currency devaluation, trade liberalization, privatization of state ventures, the creation of a commercial banking system, and removal of price controls (see item nos. 138, 151 and 152). Despite these radical measures, economic performance has been disappointing. The reduction in the civil service, from 90,000 in 1986 to 48,000 in 1995, has led to high urban unemployment and contributed to the political unrest (see item no. 149).

Mining

Up to 1990 mining was the most dynamic sector of the economy, responsible for ninety per cent of export revenues, and sixty-two per cent of domestic revenues. However, since 1990 it has suffered a decline, both in absolute and relative terms, due to technical problems, industrial disputes and growth elsewhere in the economy.

The principal mineral exploited by the mining sector is bauxite, of which Guinea possesses approximately one-third of the world's known reserves (see item nos. 157–60). The largest bauxite mine, the Boké-Sangarédi complex, some 250 km north-west of Conakry and linked by rail to Kamsar port, is operated by the Compagnie des bauxites de Guinée (CBG) (Guinea Bauxite Company). The Sangarédi reserves are likely to be exhausted by 1997, which has contributed to the drop in output in the mid-1990s. However, a new mine at nearby Bidikoum is being developed, which should help to boost production levels. The Fria site, now renamed Friguia, began processing its bauxite output into alumina in 1960, but since 1990 its production has fallen and it is undergoing a rehabilitation programme to bring it back to profitability. A third mine at Kindia, operated by the Société des bauxites de Kindia (SBK) (Kindia Bauxite Society), was developed with help from the

USSR, to whom the majority of the output was exported. The breakup of the Soviet Union has had implications for the mine, whose future now looks uncertain.

Guinea also possesses one billion tons of sixty-five to sixty-seven per cent grade iron ore (about six per cent of total world reserves) at Mount Nimba in the south-east of the country on the border with Liberia. The main barriers to the exploitation of these reserves are the inaccessibility of the area and the civil war in Liberia, which has curtailed plans to export the iron ore through the Liberian port of Buchanan.

Gold is mined both industrially and by individuals, much of the latter production not appearing in the official figures. The Société aurifère de Guinée (SAG) (Guinea Gold [mining] Society) began the exploitation in 1988 of gold deposits at Siguiri in north-east Guinea. The mine was closed in 1992, partly due to the alteration of the mining laws which allowed artisanal producers access to the site. The mine was taken over by the Australian company, Golden Shamrock, who have identified that the reserves at the site are greater than originally thought, at 2.68 million oz. The Société minière de Dinguiraye (SMD) (Dinguiraye Mining Society) began production at Léro near Siguiri in early 1995, and expects to produce 1,200 kg of high quality gold per year. The company is also optimistic about the exploitation of other reserves, particularly at Fayalala.

Diamonds are also mined both industrially and unofficially, with widespread smuggling. An estimated 80,000–125,000 carats are exported per year by individual miners, of which no more than fifteen per cent are recorded in official figures. Artisanal mining was banned in 1985 in an attempt to encourage foreign companies to invest in Guinea. The Aredor mine near Banankoro south of Kankan started production in 1984, managed by Bridge Oil of Australia. Despite early optimism, and the discovery of some of the largest diamonds found in Guinea, the venture failed to live up to expectations and was disrupted by several violent incidents. Bridge Oil pulled out in 1994 and the Aredor mine is now closed. Artisanal mining was legalized again in 1992 and these individual miners are now responsible for the bulk of Guinea's diamond production.

Agriculture

The agricultural sector contributes about seventeen per cent of GDP, with two-thirds of the population dependent for their living on agricultural activities. Guinea has the potential to grow a wide variety of crops due to its favourable and varied soil and climatic conditions, although, as with the mining sector, it has failed to live up to its potential. During Sekou Touré's government agricultural policy was based on farm collectives, with inefficient state control of resources, marketing and prices (see item no. 166). Since 1984 Lansana Conté has introduced a number of reforms, including the raising of producer prices and the abolition of production taxes (see item nos. 161 and 162). However, the farmers have been slow to respond, although production of coffee, rice and fruit have increased.

Before independence Guinea was a net exporter of food grains, but food imports now represent twice the value of agricultural exports. Despite an increase in rice output in recent years, the country imports fifty kg of rice per head per year. The other major food crops which are grown in the country are cassava, maize, yams, millet and sorghum. Exports of pineapples, mangoes and other fruit and vegetables are increasing, and cotton production is growing rapidly. Other export crops are coffee, bananas, peanuts (see item no. 163) and palm oil.

Three-quarters of the national stock of 1.7 million N'Dama cattle are kept by the Fula in the Labé and Kankan regions. Other livestock are goats, sheep, chickens and pigs, almost all kept by individual families rather than commercially.

The fisheries sector is underdeveloped (see item no. 156), with eighty per cent of the annual 100,000 ton catch coming from artisanal fishing in inland waters. Almost all offshore fish are caught by European Union boats.

Guinea has rich forest resources, which are currently only exploited for fuelwood. However, an integrated forestry industry is planned for Guinée forestière.

Other sectors of the economy

There are no known resources of fossil fuels, but the country has great potential for hydroelectric power, particularly in the Fouta Djallon region with its deep river valleys. This has been developed for the use of the alumina industry, but supplies for domestic use are totally inadequate, as only six per cent of the population receives electricity from the national grid. The principal domestic source of energy is fuelwood (see item no. 185). However, Guinea is attempting to develop the energy sector, and a major hydroelectric scheme on the Konkouré river at Garafiri is expected to be operational by 1998, despite the withdrawal of World Bank support for the scheme.

The small manufacturing sector, which accounted for only 4.5 per cent of GDP in 1993, has the principal aim of import substitution. During the Sekou Touré régime all industries were state-controlled. President Conté has introduced widespread privatization and restructuring.

The transport infrastructure has been very neglected until recently, and has been cited by the World Bank as the 'single most severe impediment to output recovery'. Before the mid-1980s the road network only served Conakry and the mining areas, but since 1985 the situation has improved, with new roads linking the capital to Kankan and other interior towns, as well as links to the rural areas, many built with foreign assistance. The railway network is also being renovated with French aid. The only public railway is from Conakry to Kankan, built at the beginning of the 20th century. The only other railways carry bauxite from Fria to Conakry and from Boké to the port of Kamsar.

Tourism is completely undeveloped in Guinea, although the government is hoping to expand hotel capacity in Conakry, and a new hotel complex was opened in 1995 at Linsan, between Kindia and Mamou.

Conclusion

Guinea has the potential to be a rich country, but due to political and economic mismanagement it has so far failed to make the most of its resources. The dark days of the Sekou Touré dictatorship are long gone, but there is still a long way to go to reach full economic development. As well as liberalizing the economy, Lansana Conté has introduced a multi-party democracy – unusual in Africa – but will he find that this becomes the cause of his downfall? The signs are not good. The opposition parties were unhappy with the legislature elections in mid-1995, and are becoming united in their opposition. There has already been a coup attempt at the beginning of 1996; can Conté hang on or will he find that he is overthrown by the democracy he has created? It must be hoped that the ethnic rivalries, which are the cause of so many conflicts in Africa, do not lead to a civil war on the scale of those in neighbouring Liberia and Sierra Leone.

The Country and Its People

1 **Africa South of the Sahara.**
London: Europa Publications, 1972- . annual.
The chapter on Guinea contains sections by recognized authorities on geography, recent history and economy, and covers agriculture, population, mining, transport and trade. Figures for population, agriculture, forestry, fishing, mining, industry, finance, trade, transport, communications and education are provided in the statistical survey. The directory section covers: the constitution; the government; political organizations; diplomatic representation; the judicial system; religion; the press; finance; trade and industry; transport; tourism; defence; and education. This continues to be a very useful source for regularly updated information.

2 **Enchantment of Africa: Guinea.**
Allan Carpenter, Thomas O'Toole.   Chicago: Children's Press, 1976.
96p.
This introductory book is aimed at schoolchildren and illustrates the geography, history, government, natural resources and people of Guinea with the aid of black-and-white photographs throughout.

3 **Guinée.** (Guinea.)
Bernard Charles.   Lausanne, Switzerland: Editions Rencontres, 1963.
223p. (L'Atlas des Voyages).
Aimed at the general reader, this illustrated book covers geography, history and customs; there are a large number of black-and-white photographs in a central section.

4 **Blende auf feur Guinea.** (Spotlight on Guinea.)
Heinz Kreuger, Joachim Umann.   Leipzig, Germany: Brockhaus,
[1961]. [unpaginated]. map.
This book of photographs, in both black-and-white and colour, is accompanied by forty pages of text in German. The photographs are mainly of smiling people, who appear to be full of optimism for the new régime under Sekou Touré.

5 **Area handbook for Guinea.**
Harold D. Nelson (et al.). Washington, DC: American University Press, 1975. 2nd ed. 386p. 10 maps. bibliog. (Foreign Area Studies, DA Pam 550-174).

Although this update of the first edition published in 1961 is now itself very out of date, it is still valuable as one of the few detailed surveys of the country in English. It is divided into four sections: social, political, economic and national security, and followed by a twenty-page bibliography divided into sections which correspond to the text.

6 **La république de Guinée.** (The republic of Guinea.)
Michel Renaudeau. Boulogne, France: Delroisse, [1977]. [20p. + unpaginated].

An official Parti démocratique de Guinée (PDG) publication which contains a collection of 176 colour plates depicting Guinea, with an introductory section of text extolling Sekou Touré's great success in developing the country. Nevertheless, the pictures are valuable as they cover every area and aspect of the country, including people, buildings, agriculture and industry.

7 **La république de Guinée.** (The republic of Guinea.)
Jean Suret-Canale. Paris: Editions Sociales, 1970. 432p. maps. bibliog.

Although now out of date, this volume remains a classic work, which is still to be replaced by a modern equivalent. It covers Guinea's geography, colonial history, commerce, agriculture, industry and communications, dealing particularly with the socio-economic developments during the first decade of the republic.

Geography

General

8   **Géographie: la république de Guinée.** (Geography: Republic of
     Guinea.)
     Alpha Mamadou Bah.   Conakry: Ministère de l'enseignement supérieur
     et tele-enseignement, 1974. 150p. 12 maps.
This is the only general geography book on Guinea. It contains sections on physical
and human geography, and also covers agriculture, forestry, minerals and industry.
The physical geography section remains the most useful, as the rest have inevitably
become dated.

9   **Guinea: Marxian socialism in a highland watershed.**
     R. J. Harrison Church.   In: *West Africa: a study of the environment and
     of man's use of it.*   London: Longman, 1974, 7th ed., p. 286-302.
Although useful for information on physical geography and climate, the section on
economic resources, which includes agriculture, mining, industry and transport,
should be treated with caution as, like so many other books on Guinea, it is now out of
date. A more recent edition of this book was published in 1983.

10   **Guinea-Liberia boundary.**
     Department of State, Office of the Geographer.   Washington, DC:
     Office of the Geographer, 1972. 5p. map. (International Boundary
     Study, no. 131).
Delineates the Guinea-Liberia boundary, which is approximately 350 miles long
(560 km) and follows the Liberian banks of various rivers as well as several straight-
line segments which are marked by pillars and monuments.

3

11 **Guinea-Senegal boundary.**
Department of State, Office of the Geographer. Washington, DC: Office of the Geographer, 1970. 3p. map. (International Boundary Study, no. 95).

A study delineating the boundary which stretches about 205 miles (330 km) east-west from Guinea-Bissau to Mali. It mostly follows rivers or straight-line segments, and is only marked by a few survey pillars.

12 **Spatial and seasonal variations of precipitable water over the Guinea-Fouta Djallon Mountains.**
Serrie I. Kamara. *Malaysian Journal of Tropical Geography*, vol. 18 (1988), p. 17-24. maps. bibliog.

The Fouta Djallon highlands have an influence on the rainfall distribution in the region. It is the second wettest area in tropical Africa after Mount Cameroon, and the high annual rainfall feeds the Niger, Senegal and Gambia rivers. This study of the precipitable water over the area looks at the spatial and temporal distribution pattern and the possible relationship to rainfall shortages. It concludes that lack of adequate moisture is not the primary cause of rainfall shortages, but rather the absence, or weakening, of mechanisms for the release of water from the atmosphere.

13 **Eléments climatologiques de la Guinée.** (Climatology of Guinea.)
Aleksander Kawalec. Conakry: Ministère de la Promotion Rurale, Service National des Sols, 1977. rev. ed. 96p. maps. bibliog.

Provides a detailed account of the climatology of Guinea and presents many explanatory maps, diagrams and photographs.

14 **Exceptional fire events in the tropics: southern Guinea.**
J. P. Malingreau, N. Laporte, J. M. Gregoire. *International Journal of Remote Sensing*, vol. 11, no. 12 (1990), p. 2,121-23. bibliog.

This short paper reports on a fire which took place on 13th January 1987, centred around the town of Kérouané. It was detected using remote sensing by the National Oceanic and Atmospheric Administration's [USA] (NOAA) Advanced Very High Resolution Radiometer (AVHRR) and was estimated to cover an area of more than 10,000 sq. km. The political boundaries of Sierra Leone and Ivory Coast show up on the image due to differences in the fire intensity, probably reflecting different land use patterns. The intensity of burning in Guinea is probably due to fires lit by pastoralists for fire regeneration, which, in the absence of tight landscape organization, went out of control. A reproduction of the coloured satellite image is included.

15 **Guinea: official standard names approved by the United States Board on Geographic Names.**
Office of Geography. Washington, DC: Office of Geography, 1965. 175p. map. (Gazetteer, no. 90).

This gazetteer contains about 12,400 entries for places and features in Guinea, listed with their latitude and longitude coordinates and the number of the administrative region in which they are located.

Maps

16   **Conakry: plan guide.** (Conakry: guide map.)
     Paris: Institut Géographique National, 1982.
This consists of two back-to-back maps, superimposed on aerial photographs, at scales of 1:10,000 and 1:15,000. The main buildings and features of the capital are named, as are the major roads.

17   **Guinea: carte générale à 1:1,000,000.** (Guinea: general map at
     1:1,000,000.)
     Paris: Institut Géographique National, 1992. 2nd ed.
A map showing areas in relief, roads, railways and forest reserves, with an inset to indicate administrative divisions. The first edition of this map was published in 1980.

18   **République de Guinée.** (Republic of Guinea.)
     Paris: Librairie Hatier, 1984.
This large (102 x 122cm) and colourful wall map consists of two back-to-back maps, at a scale of 1:700,000. One side ('Relief') is a relief map of the country, with an inset showing rainfall. The other side ('Economie') displays vegetation, agriculture, industry and minerals, with an inset revealing the industrial units in Conakry.

Geology

19 **Guinea and Sierra Leone.**
    Raymond Furon. In: *Geology of Africa.* Translated by A. Hallam, L. A.
    Stevens. Edinburgh, London: Oliver & Boyd, 1963, p. 215-21.
    Although fairly brief, this account of the geology of Guinea is the only one available
    in English. The book is a translation of the second edition of *Géologie de l'Afrique*
    (Paris: Payot, 1960), and is divided into sections on the Pre-Cambrian; Palaeozoic; the
    nepheline syenites of the Isles de Los; and the Upper Cretaceous and Palaegene of
    Portuguese Guinea. The gold, iron and diamond resources of Guinea are found in the
    Middle Pre-Cambrian. Unfortunately there is no map.

20 **Drainage basin evolution in southeast Guinea and the development
    of diamondiferous placer deposits.**
    Donald G. Sutherland. *Economic Geology*, vol. 88, no. 1 (1993),
    p. 44-54.
    Compares the evolution and diamond concentration of three contiguous drainage
    basins in south-east Guinea which contain alluvial diamond deposits. Each area has a
    distinct geomorphological history.

21 **Données paléontologiques nouvelles sur le Paléozoïque du Bassin
    Bové (Guinée, Afrique de l'Ouest): conséquences stratigraphiques.**
    (New palaeontological data from the Palaeozoic series of the Bové
    Basin [Guinea, West Africa]: stratigraphical consequences.)
    Michel Villeneuve, Mouktar C. Diallo, François Keleba, Sadamoudou
    Kourouma, Florentin Paris, Patrick R. Racheboeuf. *Comptes Rendus
    de l'Académie des Sciences, Série II*, vol. 309, no. 16 (1989),
    p. 1,583-90.
    The Bové Basin extends through Senegal, Guinea-Bissau and Guinea. This article
    reports on ten new fossiliferous localities which add significantly to the stratigraphical
    data on the Silurian succession. An English summary accompanies this French article.

Travel Guides

22 **West Africa: the rough guide.**
Jim Hudgens, Richard Trillo. London: Rough Guides, 1995. 2nd ed.
1,274p. maps.
This book is essential for anyone visiting the country, either as a tourist or on
business. The Guinea section is on p. 461-529, and contains information on travelling
into, and within, Guinea: visa requirements; money exchange; health guidelines;
transport methods; and places to eat and sleep. There is also background information
on, for example, Guinea's climate, culture and languages, and a clear, well-written
account of Guinea's history. The section on Conakry advises on places of interest,
hotels, and addresses of embassies and other important offices. There are maps of the
Kaloum Peninsula (on which Conakry is situated) and the Iles de Los, and a street
map of Conakry with all the main buildings marked. Town plans of Kindia, Mamou,
Labé, Faranah, Kissidougou and Kankan are also included, as is information on
travelling in all parts of the country. The book is outstanding in its coverage and
usefulness.

23 **West Africa: a Lonely Planet travel survival kit.**
Alex Newton, David Else. Hawthorn, Australia: Lonely Planet, 1995.
3rd ed. 924p. maps.
A very useful guidebook for anyone intending to visit the country, although not as
detailed as *West Africa: the rough guide* (q.v.). The Guinea section is on p. 441-72,
and presents information on travelling to, and around, Guinea, places to stay and eat,
and things to do. Background information on history, geography, economy, population, art, music and language is provided, and there are town plans of: Conakry,
Kindia, Mamou, Dalaba, Labé, Faranah, Kissidougou, Guéckédou, Macenta and
Kankan.

Travellers' Accounts

24 **Narrative of a journey to Musardu, the capital of the Western Mandingoes; together with: Narrative of the expedition despatched to Musahdu.**
Benjamin Anderson, with an introduction by Humphrey Fisher.
London: Frank Cass, 1971. New edition. 118 + 43p. map. (Cass Library of African Studies: Travels and Narratives, no. 69).
These narratives were originally published as two separate books in 1870 and 1912. They present accounts of two expeditions in 1868-69 and 1874, travelling from the Liberian capital, Monrovia, along the St Pauls River into present-day Guinea in search of Musardu, the capital of the Malinké (Mandingoes). Musardu is probably the present-day Moussadougou, north of Beyla.

25 **De l'Atlantique au Niger par le Foutah-Djallon.** (From the Atlantic to Niger via the Fouta Djallon.)
Aimé Olivier Vicomte de Sanderval. Paris: Ducrocq, 1882. 407p. map.
An account of a journey undertaken in 1879-80 from the Atlantic Coast to Timbo, the Islamic capital of the Fouta Djallon, and back again. The route taken on the outward leg was along the Rio Grande and the River Cassim, while the return itinerary took a more southerly course, arriving back at the coast via the Rio Nunez. Taken from the author's diary, this is a very detailed account of his travels and the people and sights he encountered along the way, illustrated throughout with copper plate engravings. It includes records of temperature and barometric pressure, and the exact times of events and departures.

26 **Les rives du Konkouré: de l'Atlantique au Foutah-Djalon.** (The banks of the Konkouré: from the Atlantic to the Fouta Djallon.)
Comte de Sanderval. Paris: Challamel, 1900. 30p. + [18p.] 2 maps.
This account of a voyage of exploration along the Konkouré River is accompanied by some fascinating historical photographs. The journey was undertaken in order to

assess the possibility of running a railway from Conakry to Niger, and a map of the proposed route is included. The account and photographs provide an insight into the methods employed, and the levels of comfort expected, by European explorers at the end of the 19th century.

27 **Narrative of Mr William Cooper Thompson's journey from Sierra Leone to Timbo, capital of Futah Jallo in Western Africa.**
Lord Stanley. *Journal of the Royal Geographical Society*, vol. 16 (1846), p. 106-38.
An account of the journey by William Thompson, who set out in December 1841 in order to set up trading links between Sierra Leone and the Islamic state of Fouta Djallon. Unfortunately, after his arrival at Timbo in June 1842, he was virtually kept prisoner for nearly eighteen months and died there in November 1843. Some of the account is written in the first person, taken from Thompson's diary, while the rest is narrated by Lord Stanley.

The sacred forest: the fetishist and magic rites of the Toma.
See item no. 97.

Flora and Fauna

28 **Flore et végétation de la lisière de la forêt dense en Guinée.** (Flora and vegetation at the margin of the dense forest in Guinea.)
J. G. Adam. *Bulletin de l'Institut Fondamental d'Afrique Noire, Series A,* vol. 30, no. 3 (1968), p. 920-52. map. bibliog.

Examines the vegetation in the area of the source of the Milo, a tributary of the River Niger. It lists all the plants identified in the area and presents an alphabetical list of species and their locations.

29 **Les poissons du Fouta Dialon et de la Basse Guinée.** (The fish of the Fouta Djallon and Lower Guinea.)
J. Daget. Dakar: Institut Français d'Afrique Noire, 1962. 210p. maps. bibliog. (Mémoires de l'Institut Français d'Afrique Noire, no. 65).

An account of the fish to be found in the rivers of the Fouta Djallon. The first part has details of rainfall, the chemicals to be found in the water and recorded water temperatures, while the bulk of the book consists of detailed descriptions of the fish species, many of which are illustrated with line drawings. The last section provides bio-geographical information on the various river basins. Thirty-two black-and-white photographs at the end of the book illustrate some of the species and locations.

30 **Essai sur la flore de la Guinée Française.** (Essay on the flora of French Guinea.)
H. Pobéguin. Paris: Challamel, 1906. 392p. map.

This extremely detailed account of the plants of Guinea is illustrated with eighty black-and-white photographic plates throughout the text. An introductory chapter is followed by a chapter on forest products, agricultural products and the cultivation by Europeans of garden flowers and vegetables. The main part of the book provides descriptions of the native flora classed by family. There are lists of Latin names and the names of plants in native languages.

31   The flora of Bossou: its utilization by chimpanzees and humans.
Yukimaru Sugiyama, Jeremy Koman.   *African Study Monographs*, vol.
13, no. 3 (1992), p. 127-69.

The authors have identified and listed 664 plant species from 392 genera, growing in the Bossou region in the south-eastern corner of Guinea. They have examined the ways in which chimpanzees and man use many of the plants: chimpanzees use 246 items from 200 different plants for food, while humans use only 83 items from 76 plants for food; however, people also use 113 items from 81 species for traditional medicine. Plants are also needed for house and furniture construction, as well as for other uses. The authors wish to draw attention to the importance of the various plant species, as deforestation is reducing the areas of primary forest in this region.

L'originalité des mangroves de Guinée dans le monde tropical humide.
(The uniqueness of the mangroves of Guinea in the humid tropics.)
See item no. 178.

Whose social forestry and why? People, trees and managed continuity in Guinea's forest-savanna mosaic.
See item no. 182.

History

General

32 **Lexique historique de la Guinée-Conakry.** (Historical glossary of
Guinea.)
Aly Gilbert Iffono.   Paris: L'Harmattan, 1992. 234p. bibliog. (Racines
du Présent).

This useful book provides descriptions and explanations of historical figures and
events, listed alphabetically. Included in the appendices are: a chronological history of
Guinea from 1818 to 1991; genealogical tables of the almami who ruled the Fouta
Djallon; the texts of treaties with France; the statutes of the Parti démocratique de
Guinée (PDG); speeches by General de Gaulle and Sekou Touré on the occasion of de
Gaulle's visit to Guinea in 1958; a list of the victims of the notorious Camp Boiro
prison camp; the names of the political parties registered in 1992; and a short history
of Guinean literature.

33 **Historical dictionary of Guinea (Republic of Guinea/Conakry).**
Thomas E. O'Toole.   Metuchen, New Jersey; London: Scarecrow,
1987. 2nd ed. 204p. bibliog. (African Historical Dictionaries, no. 16).

This update of the original 1978 edition contains a very useful chronology of major
events up to 1986, while the dictionary itself provides explanations and information
about names and terminology associated with Guinea. The bibliography section
comprises some seventy-five pages of references to books and articles in English and
French, and is divided into broad subject headings covering history, economy,
scientific studies, religion, literature, art and music.

34 **Colonialism and the African nation: the case of Guinea.**
Peter M. Slowe. In: *Colonialism and development in the contemporary world.* Edited by Chris Dixon, Michael J. Heffernan. London: Mansell, 1991, p. 106-20. bibliog.
This paper seeks to show that each stage in Guinea's history has offered a different approach to development. Before the French colonized and imposed their own boundaries on the area now known as Guinea, the area had been dominated by the kingdom of Fouta Djallon and the Malinké empire. Following an examination of the latter period, Slowe goes on to deal with the colonial era and the subsequent rejection of the French by Sekou Touré, who sought to impose a socialist system on the country. Finally, the author examines Lansana Conté's attempts to reconstruct the economy since 1985.

Pre-colonial

35 **An 1804 slaving contract signed in Arabic script from the Upper Guinea coast.**
George E. Brooks, Bruce L. Mouser. *History in Africa*, vol. 14 (1987), p. 341-47.
Few slaving contracts have survived, but this article discusses a contract dated 15th November 1804, negotiated aboard the American merchant ship, *Charlotte,* anchored at the Iles de Los off Conakry. It is signed in Arabic by Dumbuya, a Soussou who ruled the coastal area at the time, who agreed to pay in rice and slaves for the ship's cargo of rum, tobacco and other goods.

36 **Les institutions politiques du Fouta-Dyalon au XIXe siècle.** (Political institutions of the Fouta Djallon in the 19th century.)
Thierno Diallo. Dakar: Institut Fondamental d'Afrique Noire, 1972. 276p. 3 maps. bibliog. (Institutions et Etudes Africaines, no. 28).
Originally a thesis presented at the University of Paris, this is an extremely detailed history of the Fouta Djallon, its tribes and their conflicts, which covers the social structure and evolution, and pre-colonial administrative organization. It includes: genealogical and chronological tables of the almami, the Islamic chiefs who held supreme power in the Fouta Djallon in the 19th century, whose title was abolished by the French in 1912; a list of the principal European explorers of the Fouta Djallon in the 19th century; and a lexicon of Fula (Peul) words.

37 **'Two hippos cannot live in one river.' Zo Musa, Foningama, and the founding of Musadu in the oral traditions of the Konyaka.**
Tim Geysbeek, Jobba K. Kamara. *Liberian Studies Journal*, vol. 16, no. 1 (1991), p. 27-78.
Examines the oral traditions relating to the founding of the town of Musardu in south-east Guinea. Zo Musa was a Guerzé slave who settled in the area and emerged as

leader of the local people, but was forced to flee by the Malinké led by Foningama. The authors list the many versions of the story which have been collected by travellers and researchers since the 19th century, although the majority have been collected during the 1980s. It is a story that transmits much information about moral and social values and political power in pre-colonial Guinea. The paper also includes genealogical charts of Foningama's ancestry and descendants.

38 **Big men, traders, and chiefs: power, commerce and spatial change in the Sierra Leone-Guinea plain, 1865-1895.**
Allen M. Howard. PhD thesis, University of Wisconsin, Wisconsin, 1972. 477p. bibliog.

The second half of the 19th century was a time between the end of the slave trade and the imposition of colonialism, when relationships with Europe, largely based on trade, were being worked out. This thesis focuses on the main trade corridors and the coastal belt of the Guinea-Sierra Leone area, and the power struggles between the main tribal chiefs who were all trying to gain the best trading advantages.

39 **Trade and politics in the Nunez and Pongo Rivers, 1790-1865.**
Bruce Lee Mouser. PhD thesis, Indiana University, Indiana, 1971; Ann Arbor, Michigan: University Microfilms, 1975. 320p.

The Rio Nunez and Rio Pongo on the Guinea coast are two of a number of rivers which have their source in the Fouta Djallon highlands. The slave trade along these routes was important during the 18th century, but by the beginning of the 19th century the trade had become illegal, and there was a gradual transition to legitimate commerce. Moreover, the introduction of coffee and peanuts for export had hastened the end of the Atlantic slave trade, for the slaves were now employed domestically on the plantations. This very detailed thesis analyses the interaction between traders and chiefs, and the contrasting reactions in the two areas.

40 **Women slavers of Guinea-Conakry.**
Bruce Lee Mouser. In: *Women and slavery in Africa.* Edited by Claire C. Robertson, Martin A. Klein. Madison, Wisconsin: University of Wisconsin Press, 1983, p. 320-39.

During the late 18th and early 19th centuries a number of women were active participants in the slave trade. Three in particular became very well known: Betsy Heard, Elizabeth Frazer Skelton and Mary Faber, and sections of this chapter are devoted to each of these. They were all well educated and aspired to a European lifestyle. They came to have great influence on the commerce of the Guinea area.

41 **The Atlantic coast and the southern savannahs 1800-1880.**
Yves Person. In: *History of West Africa.* Edited by J. F. A. Ajayi, Michael Crowder. London: Longman, 1987, 2nd ed., p. 250-300.

During the 19th century the Fouta Djallon was an important and powerful kingdom that controlled trade along the West African coastal area. It was the slave trade that brought the greatest wealth. Discussed in this chapter are the leaders of the Fouta Djallon and the power struggles which led up to the reign of its most famous leader, Samori Touré, who was instrumental in resisting the French advance.

42 **Samori, une révolution dyula.** (Samori, a Dyula revolution.)
Yves Person. Dakar: Institut Fondamental d'Afrique Noire, 1968-75.
3 vols. (Mémoires de IFAN, nos. 80 & 89).

This work comprises three huge volumes, totalling 2,377 pages, which detail the rise of the Malinké chief, Samori Touré, and his struggles against the French and other tribal leaders. During the period 1870-75 Samori waged a number of raids and military operations against the many tribes of the Fouta Djallon who had been torn apart by continuous warfare. After capturing Kankan in 1879 he set up his capital at Bissandugu and consolidated his rule over the area. He organized his kingdom into ten provincial governments, each administered by a loyal friend or relative, who collected taxes and dispensed justice. From 1891 onwards, as the French attempted to establish colonial rule, Samori mobilized his warriors to fight a succession of expeditionary forces. However, in September 1898 he was finally captured in a surprise attack at Guélémou and deported to Gabon, where he died in 1900. The book contains a wealth of detail about the administration of Samori's kingdom and the traditional way of life in pre-colonial Guinea.

43 **On the veracity of oral tradition as a historical source; the case of Somori Ture.**
Stanislaw Pilaszewicz. In: *Unwritten testimonies of the African past.*
Edited by S. Pilaszewicz, E. Rzewuski. Warsaw: University of Warsaw, Institute of Oriental Studies, 1991, p. 167-80. bibliog.
(Orientalia Varsoviensia, no. 2).

Samori Touré (c.1830-1900) was a great Malinké warrior and state-builder, claimed as an ancestor by Sekou Touré. This article is concerned with the use of oral sources as a tool in historical research, and the reliability of such sources compared with written accounts. The main written sources from the time were accounts by French army officers who were trying to capture the area and suffered defeats at the hand of Samori, who had created a strong kingdom. For the African side of this story it is necessary to use oral sources. The article analyses two texts which are written accounts of oral traditions, and compares the information about Samori which is provided in both of them.

44 **A history of the Upper Guinea coast 1545-1800.**
Walter Rodney. Oxford: Clarendon Press, 1970. 283p. 5 maps.
bibliog.

This book, which is a revised version of the author's doctoral thesis, covers the area of West Africa from Gambia to Cape Mount, Liberia, including the Guinea coastal plain and the area inland up to the edge of the Fouta Djallon. The whole of this part of West Africa was known as Guinea before being partitioned into the various English, French and Portuguese colonies. The period covered by the book is the time when African society was still largely free of European influence, but by 1800 the coastal societies had been overwhelmed by forces set in motion by the slave trade.

Bokar Biro: le dernier grand almamy du Fouta Djallon. (Bokar Biro: the last great almami of the Fouta Djallon.)
See item no. 85.

Révolte, pouvoir, religion: les Hubbu de Futa-Jalon (Guinée). (Revolt, power, religion: the Hubbu of Fouta Djallon [Guinea].)
See item no. 110.

L'Islam en Guinée: Fouta-Diallon. (Islam in Guinea: Fouta Djallon.)
See item no. 111.

The guardian of the word.
See item no. 192.

Colonial period

45 **La Guinée française: races, religions, coutumes, production, commerce.** (French Guinea: races, religions, customs, production, commerce.)
André Arçin. Paris: Challamel, 1907. 659p. 4 maps.

A detailed and fascinating account of the country at the beginning of the colonial period. It covers: the geography; climate; economy; social organization and ethnic groups; government and politics; customs and rituals; Islam; and the French administration, with black-and-white photographs throughout. Two appendices list the administrative divisions and present some information about the various languages. The author was a colonial administrator in the office of the governor of Guinea, and wrote another book: *Histoire de la Guinée française* (History of French Guinea) (Paris: Challamel, 1911).

46 **Guinea: the years before World War II: an historical sketch and a bibliographic appendix of 112 titles.**
Victor D. Du Bois. *American Universities Field Staff (AUFS) Reports: West Africa Series*, vol. 5, no. 5 (1962), p. 53-72. bibliog.

This is the first of four papers by the same author which discuss the years leading up to Guinea's independence, and the problems and prospects for the newly-independent country as it faced the future free from the constraints and oppression of colonialism, but without the economic support offered by the French. The other papers in the same volume of the series are: 'Guinea's prelude to independence' (no. 6, p. 73-88); 'The Guinean vote for independence' (no. 7, p. 89-101); and 'The problems of independence' (no. 8, p. 103-20).

47 **Commerce et colonisation en Guinée, 1850-1913.** (Commerce and colonization in Guinea, 1850-1913.)
Odile Goerg. Paris: L'Harmattan, 1986. 431p. 12 maps. bibliog. (Racines du Présent).

The French authorities asserted their influence as colonizers in order to control the trading economy. This book looks at this relationship between trade and colonialism, using the rubber trade as an illustration.

48 **La genèse du peuplement de Conakry.** (Conakry's population in the
early days.)
Odile Goerg. *Cahiers d'Études Africaines*, vol. 30, no. 1 (1990),
p. 73-99. bibliog.

This paper, which is in French with an English abstract, examines the settlement of
Conakry during its initial phase (1885-1910), with respect to the ethnic identity of the
immigrants who joined the existing population, and the colonial authorities' attitudes
towards these immigrants. The population was characterized, as it still is today, by a
predominance of Soussou and Fula (Peul), many of whom came from the hinterland
and other French African possessions. This article is related to another by the same
author: 'Conakry: un modèle de ville coloniale française? Règlements fonciers et
urbanisme de 1885 aux années 1920 (Conakry: a model for the French colonial town?
Land rights and town planning from 1885 to the 1920s), *Cahiers d'Études Africaines*,
vol. 25, no. 3 (1985), p. 309-35, which looks at the planning of Conakry by the
French.

49 **Sierra Leoneans in Guinea: an introduction.**
Odile Goerg. In: *Sierra Leone studies at Birmingham 1988.* Edited
by Adam Jones, Peter K. Mitchell, Margaret Peil. Birmingham,
England: University of Birmingham, 1990, p. 7-20. bibliog.

Before the imposition of colonial rule in West Africa, there was free movement in the
coastal hinterland for trading purposes. Many Sierra Leonean traders settled in
Guinea, where they helped to build the town of Conakry and introduced the Protestant
religion. However, there was growing rivalry between the French and British as they
vied for territory and trading partners. This study researches the treatment by the
French colonial authorities of Sierra Leoneans who had settled in Conakry. Their
English-speaking influence was distrusted by the French, who often used them as
scapegoats and accused them of slave trading. Although they remained a distinct
community, Sierra Leoneans gradually became marginalized as Conakry grew in size.

50 **La Guinée française.** (French Guinea.)
Maurice Houis. Paris: Éditions Maritimes et Coloniales, 1953. 95p. 4
maps. bibliog. (Pays Africains, no. 3).

Written during the French colonial era, this book presents a general overview of the
country at that time. There are chapters on geography, ethnic groups, religion, history,
politics, society, agriculture, industry, economy and tourism, together with several
black-and-white photographs.

51 **Le 'Non' de la Guinée à de Gaulle.** (Guinea's 'No' to de Gaulle.)
Lansiné Kaba. Paris: Editions Chaka, [1990]. 190p. bibliog.

On 28th September 1958 the people of Guinea voted overwhelmingly to reject the
proposal of the Fifth Republic, under which the French colonies would become part of
a French African community. This book looks in detail at the events leading up to this
end to the colonial government, and examines the influence of Sekou Touré, who was
secretary-general of the Parti démocratique de Guinée (PDG) and became the first
president of independent Guinea.

52 **Slave resistance and slave emancipation in coastal Guinea.**
Martin A. Klein. In: *The end of slavery in Africa.* Edited by Suzanne
Miers, Richard Roberts. Madison, Wisconsin: University of
Wisconsin Press, 1988, p. 203-19.

The Rio Nunez on the Guinea coast was for four centuries a base for slave-trading operations. The end of the Atlantic slave trade did not end the trading of slaves within West Africa. The slave labour was used in the production of peanuts and other export crops. This paper discusses the revolt in 1908 by slaves who had been brought to the coast to produce peanuts. The French colonial authorities felt that although freeing slaves was politically desirable, commodity production would be affected.

53 **Le chemin de fer de Konakry au Niger (1890-1914).** (The railway
from Conakry to the Niger 1890-1914.)
Jacques Mangotte. *Revue Française d'Histoire d'Outre-Mer*, vol. 55,
no. 198 (1968), p. 37-105.

A railway was constructed by the French, from Conakry to the River Niger, in order to facilitate trade and strengthen French colonial control over the Rivières du Sud, as Guinea was known at the time. This paper uses records of research from the colonial archives to detail the route chosen and the stages in the construction of the railway. It also assesses the effects on Guinea's trade.

54 **L'avenir de la Guinée française.** (The future of French Guinea.)
Roland Pre. Paris: Lescaret, 1951. 280p. maps.

Written by the French Governor of Guinea at the time, this looks at the prospects for Guinea in the light of its possible future independence. It provides a detailed account of the agriculture, mineral resources, hydroelectric potential, industrialization and the possible development of ports for the export of products.

55 **World War I conscription and social change in Guinea.**
Anne Summers, R. W. Johnson. *Journal of African History*, vol. 19,
no. 1 (1978), p. 25-38.

Military conscription was introduced by France to Guinea in 1912, as a means of training a local administrative corps to replace the traditional chiefs who still resisted colonial authority. However, the chiefs were still powerful in 1914, and their help was sought in recruiting between 20,000 and 30,000 conscripts during the First World War. This article discusses the problems caused by the return of the *ancien combattants* (former soldiers) after the war. They had been influenced by their contact with French socialists, and they remained a distinct social grouping between the wars, who conflicted with the chiefs.

56 **Guinea in the colonial system.**
Jean Suret-Canale. In: *Essays on African history: from the slave trade
to neocolonialism.* Translated from the French by Christopher Hurst.
London: Hurst, 1988, p. 111-47.

A useful account of colonialism in Guinea, which is only really known from official records of expeditions and conquests, and not usually from the point of view of the ordinary Guinean people. The coastal region of the Rivières du Sud was the first area to be annexed by the French in 1890, but the Fouta Djallon held out longer, and the present frontiers only came into being in 1899. The second part of the paper deals with colonization once the boundaries had been fixed, and includes sections on rubber production, the persistence of slavery, and the issue of chieftainship. Overall, the colonial system is regarded as being unfavourable to the mass of the population. This paper was first published in French as 'La Guinée dans le système colonial' (*Présence Africaine*, vol. 29 [1959], p. 9-44), translated as 'Guinea under the colonial system' (*Présence Africaine, English Edition*, vol. 1, no. 29 [1960], p. 21-62).

Alfa Yaya, roi du Labé. (Alfa Yaya, king of Labé.)
See item no. 86.

Tcherno Aliou, the Wali of Goumba: Islam, colonialism and the rural factor in Futa Jallon, 1867-1912.
See item no. 112.

Bibliographie critique des sources imprimées de l'histoire de la Guinée publiées avant 1914. (Annotated bibliography of printed sources on the history of Guinea published before 1914.)
See item no. 223.

Sekou Touré government (1958-84)

57 **Sékou Touré's Guinea: an experiment in nation building.**
    Ladipo Adamolekun.   London: Methuen, 1976. 250p. bibliog. (Studies in African History, no. 12).

Written before the atrocities of Sekou Touré's régime came to light, this book seeks to analyse Guinea's chances of success in its attempts to transform itself into a socialist state. The author identifies the major factors in the Guinean approach to nation building as being the political institutional framework, the programme of socio-economic development and the quest for a national identity; and the major factors in pursuing this as being a mobilization-oriented single party, an inflexible party ideology, and a flexible and charismatic leader. It is interesting to read this optimistic account of Sekou Touré and his policies in the light of what is now known about the devastation he caused to the country's economy.

58 **La Guinée: bilan d'une indépendance.** (Guinea: assessment of an independence.)
    B. Ameillon.   Paris: François Maspero, 1964. 205p.

Writing not long after independence, Ameillon examines Guinea's relations with France and the rest of the world. Questions posed relate to the direction Sekou Touré's régime was taking and whether independence would succeed. The author also assesses the development of Guinean society prior to 1958 and the effects of the end of chieftaincy.

59 **Guinea.**
Amnesty International.   London: Amnesty International, 1978. 12p.
(Amnesty International Briefing Papers, no. 14).
Amnesty International seeks to bring to public attention issues of the violation of
human rights. This account describes the widespread use of prolonged detention of
political prisoners, often without trial, and the harsh conditions and torture that many
suffered during Sekou Touré's régime. After the publication of this report and in
response to criticism from the international community, the Guinean government
began a process of liberalization and claimed that such abuses of human rights had
ceased.

60 **The political thought of Sékou Touré.**
Charles E. Andrain.   In: *African political thought: Lumumba,*
Nkrumah, and Touré.   Edited by W. A. E. Skurnik.   Denver,
Colorado: University of Denver, 1968, p. 101-47. (Monograph Series in
World Affairs, vol. 5, nos. 3 & 4).
Represents an uncritical examination of President Touré's writings and speeches, and
a discussion of his political ideology. The author states that Touré held a monistic
view of reality, condemning both individualism and pluralism, and seeing a need to
synthesize modern values of economic organization with pre-colonial African values
of communal solidarity.

61 **The reds and the blacks: a personal adventure.**
William Attwood.   London: Hutchinson, 1967. 341p.
Presents an Amerocentric view of post-independence Guinea, at the time when Guinea
was in the throes of the communist/socialist revolution. The author was an American
ambassador, working in both Guinea and Kenya. He presents a personal account of the
political manoeuvrings between America, and the communist powers of Russia and
China who were pouring aid into Guinea at the time, in an attempt to gain valuable
trading relations. See also *First American ambassador to Guinea* by John Henry
Morrow (q.v.).

62 **Camp Boiro: sinistre geôle de Sékou Touré.** (Camp Boiro: Sekou
Touré's sinister jail.)
Ardo Ousmane Bâ.   Paris: L'Harmattan, 1986. 276p. (Memoires
Africaines).
This presents a day-to-day account of life in the appalling conditions of Camp Boiro
prison camp, where the author was a political prisoner from 1973 to 1978. A similar
book by Jean-Paul Alata, *Prison d'Afrique* (African prison) (Paris: Editions du Seuil,
1976), gives an account of five years spent in Guinean jails.

63 **Construire la Guinée après Sékou Touré.** (Rebuilding Guinea after
Sekou Touré.)
Mahmoud Bah.   Paris: L'Harmattan, 1990. 207p. map.
The author, who was imprisoned by Sekou Touré from 1979 to 1984, presents an
account of the atrocities committed against the people of Guinea during Sekou

Touré's reign of terror. It also assesses what the future holds for Guinea after Sekou Touré's death.

64   **Guinée: Albanie d'Afrique ou néo-colonie americaine.** (Guinea: Albania of Africa or American neo-colony.)
Alpha Conde.   Paris: Git Le Coeur, 1972. 270p.
Argues that far from being a model socialist state (the 'Albania of Africa'), Guinea had become an American neo-colony, with Sekou Touré, paranoid about political opposition, under the protection of the CIA. It follows the political history of Guinea through from French colonization, to independence, and the subsequent subjugation of the people. It paints a very critical picture of Touré and his motives.

65   **Guinée enchainée ou le livre noir de Sékou Touré.** (Guinea in chains or Sekou Touré's black book.)
Claude Abou Diakité.   [s.l.]: [n.p.], 1972. 266p.
This book criticises Sekou Touré's régime for its: oppression of all opposition; mistreatment and execution of political prisoners; and maladministration of the Guinean economy.

66   **La mort de Diallo Telli: premier secrétaire général de l'O.A.U.** (The death of Diallo Telli: first secretary general of the O.A.U.)
Amadou Diallo.   Paris: Karthala, 1983. 154p.
The author was a fellow prisoner of Diallo Telli in Boiro prison camp during Sekou Touré's dictatorship. He includes a plan of the camp, and presents a graphic account of life there. An appendix lists seventy-eight prisoners, and is illustrated with photographs taken in the prison camp; all these men were arrested between 1969 and 1976 and 'disappeared' in prison. There is an extract from the Amnesty International report on the abuse of human rights in Guinea (q.v.). See also *Diallo Telli: le tragique destin d'un grand Africain* by André Lewin (q.v.).

67   **The significance of Guinea's independence.**
Georges Fischer.   *Présence Africaine, English Edition*, vol. 1, no. 29 (1960), p. 11-20.
Written for a journal published to celebrate Guinea's independence, this article views Sekou Touré's revolution as the key to Guinea's economic success, now that the country had been freed from the bonds of colonialism.

68   **Guinée, état-pilote.** (Guinea, pilot state.)
Fernand Gigon.   Paris: Plon, 1959. 109p. (Tribune Libre, no. 51).
This book, written just after independence, includes an interview with Sekou Touré and looks optimistically towards Guinea's future now it was free from the exploitation of colonialism and eager to pursue its own socialist policies under a charismatic leader.

69 **Guinée: prélude à l'indépendance.** (Guinea: prelude to independence.) Paris: Présence Africaine, 1958. 175p.

Presents a transcript of the meeting, held in 1957, which led to the abolition of the traditional chiefs, and ultimately to the 'no' vote rejecting French rule. The discussions, led by Sekou Touré, are reproduced verbatim. See also *The end of chieftaincy in Guinea* by Jean Suret-Canale (q.v.).

70 **L'impérialisme et sa 5ème colonne en République de Guinée: agression de 22 Novembre 1970.** (Imperialism and its 5th column in the Republic of Guinea: the attack of 22nd November 1970.) [Conakry]: Imprimerie Nationale, 1971. 701p.

A collection of 'confessions' by people supposedly involved in the attack of 22nd November 1970, in which Portuguese-led troops attacked Conakry from the sea in an attempt to topple Sekou Touré. The book begins with two messages from Sekou Touré to the nation, condemning the 'imperialist' aggression. The confessions and statements are accompanied by pictures of the accused taken in prison camps.

71 **From colonialism to autocracy: Guinea under Sékou Touré, 1957-1984.** Lansiné Kaba. In: *Decolonization and African independence: the transfers of power, 1960-1980.* Edited by Prosser Gifford, W. Roger Louis. New Haven, Connecticut: Yale University Press, 1988, p. 225-44.

This paper assesses the period of Sekou Touré's rule following the sudden transfer of power from the French. Touré commanded great popular support at first with his socialist revolution, but he became increasingly autocratic, and only remained in power by the repression of all opposition.

72 **Ahmed Sekou Touré: l'homme de 28 Septembre 1958.** (Ahmed Sekou Touré: the man of 28th September 1958.) Sidiki Kobele Keita. Conakry: Bibliothèque Nationale, 1977. 2nd ed. 136p.

Provides a detailed chronology of the events leading up to, and immediately following, independence in 1958. Sekou Touré is portrayed as a great hero of the people. There are black-and-white photographs throughout.

73 **First American ambassador to Guinea.** John Henry Morrow. New Brunswick, New Jersey: Rutgers University Press, 1968. 291p.

An autobiographical account by John Morrow who, in 1959, while working as a college professor, was told that he had been chosen to represent the United States in the new Republic of Guinea. While in Guinea, from July 1959 to March 1961, he witnessed and participated in many of Sekou Touré's dealings with foreign governments, at the time when the new president was aligning himself increasingly with the communist governments of Eastern Europe. Morrow is critical of the American government's approach to Guinea: he felt that they should give aid to

Guinea in spite of the communist presence. See also *The reds and the blacks* by William Attwood (q.v.).

74 **Revolution in Africa.**
Kavalan Madhu Panikkar. Bombay: Asia Publishing House, 1961. 202p.
This represents one of the most important books in English on Guinea's independence. It is divided into two parts: part one (p. 3-135), 'Nationalism and the rise of nation states', examines the issues leading to the rise of nationalism in the African colonies; part two (p. 139-93), 'Guinea: a case study', concentrates on the factors leading to revolution and independence in Guinea. Sekou Touré is regarded as a remarkable leader whose policies led Guinea out of the grip of colonial domination.

75 **Révolution Démocratique Africaine.** (African Democratic Revolution.)
Conakry: [n.p.], [1964]-1984. irregular.
A series of over 200 numbered books and pamphlets, published by the government of Guinea, the majority being by Sekou Touré. Many are speeches given by the President, or reports of state visits and other official occasions. Although, by its nature, much of the material is propaganda, historians will find many items of interest.

76 **Guinea: the mobilization of a people.**
Claude Rivière, translated from French by Virginia Thompson, Richard Adloff. Ithaca, New York: Cornell University Press, 1977. 262p. map. bibliog. (Africa in the Modern World).
Written during Sekou Touré's period of leadership, this book examines the political and economic history and development of Guinea, describing the economic and social transformations that had taken place since 1958. Four of the seven chapters appeared previously in *Revue Française d'Etudes Politiques Africaines*. The author has written extensively on Guinea.

77 **Social origins of the 1984 coup d'etat in Guinea.**
George Rubiik. *Utafiti: Journal of the Faculty of Arts and Social Sciences, University of Dar es Salaam*, vol. 9, no. 1 (1987), p. 93-118.
Focuses on the background to the 1984 coup in which the right-wing military overthrew the socialist civilian government following Sekou Touré's sudden death. It concludes that the revolutionary myth of Sekou Touré paralysed all other institutions apart from the army. This is one of the few analyses of this event.

78 **The French press and Guinea.**
Léonard Sainville. *Présence Africaine, English Edition*, vol. 1, no. 29 (1960), p. 121-29.
Surveys the opinions of the French press on Guinea's first year of independence. The overwhelming theme seems to be that France was afraid Guinea had turned away from them towards the communist East, which might use Guinea as a pawn in the Cold War.

79 **Sékou Touré.**
London: Panaf, 1978. 208p. (Panaf Great Lives Series).
Rather than being simply a biography of Sekou Touré, this book presents an account of his policies and achievements. Some historical background is provided, with Sekou Touré claiming descent from Samori Touré, the great 19th-century Guinean leader who resisted the French colonization. Although no author is credited, Sekou Touré himself appears to have had quite a large hand in the writing of this book which is very positive about his achievements. There are two militant poems by him and a chronology of important dates in the history of the Parti démocratique de Guinée (PDG) from 1947 to 1977.

80 **The end of chieftaincy in Guinea.**
Jean Suret-Canale. In: *Essays on African history: from the slave trade to neocolonialism.* Translated from the French by Christopher Hurst.
London: Hurst, 1988, p. 148-78.
The chieftaincy system had been introduced by the French at the end of the 19th century in an attempt to obtain the loyalty of traditional leaders by vesting in them administrative and judicial powers. Chiefs who opposed the colonizing power were removed, and the previous symbols of authority, such as the title 'almami' were abolished. However, the system was widely abused and corrupt and was regarded by the Guinean people as signifying their oppression. The chieftaincy system was officially abolished by a decree of 31st December 1957, which enabled the PDG under Sekou Touré to smooth the path towards independence. This paper, by an influential writer on Guinean affairs, originally appeared as 'La fin de la chefferie en Guinée' (*Journal of African History*, vol. 7, no. 3 [1966], p. 459-93). It also appeared in *African politics and society: basic issues and problems of government and development*, edited by Irving Leonard Markovitz (New York: The Free Press, 1970, p. 96-117).

81 **Africa on the move.**
Ahmed Sekou Touré. London: Panaf, 1979. 607p.
Sekou Touré presents his definition of the Guinean revolution and the aims, objectives and ideology of the Democratic Party of Guinea (PDG). Socialism is presented as the answer to exploitation. Sekou Touré wrote many books in French proclaiming his views, but this is one of the few to be translated into English.

82 **Guinean revolution and social progress.**
Ahmed Sekou Touré. Cairo: S.O.P. Press, [1963]. 448p.
One of a huge number of books by Sekou Touré putting forward his revolutionary ideas. He presents the historical background to the Guinean revolution and the formation of the PDG, followed by chapters on education, economic development, foreign policy and national institutions, which claim achievements and announce plans for the future. An appendix reproduces some documents relating to the Organisation of African Unity. This was written at a time of great optimism in Guinea and is presented in the language of political propaganda.

83 **Guinée: unique survivant du 'Complot Kaman-Fodeba'.** (Guinea: sole survivor of the 'Kaman-Fodeba plot'.)
Kindo Touré. Paris: L'Harmattan, 1989. 194p. (Memoires Africaines).
The author was accused of involvement in the so-called Labé plot in 1969, one of many supposed plots to overthrow Sekou Touré, who became increasingly paranoid as his presidency wore on. This recounts the author's time in various prison camps, including Kindia and the notorious Camp Boiro. He was finally freed in 1984.

84 **Report of the Security Council Special Mission to the Republic of Guinea established under Resolution 289 (1970).**
United Nations, Security Council. New York: United Nations, 1971. 213p. (Security Council Official Records, 25th Year, Special Supplement, no. 2).
A detailed report of the United Nations Special Mission sent to Guinea at the request of Sekou Touré to investigate the attack on Conakry by Portuguese mercenary troops on 22nd November 1970. During the night of 21st/22nd November a number of troops came ashore from boats moored off Conakry. They attacked the Presidential Palace and the headquarters of the Partido Africano para la Independência da Guiné e Cabo Verde (PAIGC), which was fighting from a base in Conakry for the independence of Portuguese Guinea. The troops also freed a number of political prisoners and took them back to the ships, which then departed. The Mission concludes that the troops were indeed Portuguese-led from Guinea-Bissau, and included a number of Guinean dissidents. The report includes verbatim records of interviews with witnesses.

Sékou Touré: le héros et le tyran. (Sekou Touré: the hero and the tyrant.)
See item no. 88.

Diallo Telli: le tragique destin d'un grand Africain. (Diallo Telli: the tragic destiny of a great African.)
See item no. 89.

Guinea.
See item no. 125.

Guinea: united against the world.
See item no. 128.

The Parti Démocratique de Guinée and the Mamou 'deviation'.
See item no. 129.

Guinea: a challenge to American foreign policy.
See item no. 135.

Un week-end à Conakry. (A weekend in Conakry.)
See item no. 195.

Biography and Autobiography

85 **Bokar Biro: le dernier grand almami du Fouta Djallon.** (Bokar Biro:
the last great almami of the Fouta Djallon.)
Boubacar Barry.   Paris: ABC; Dakar, Abidjan: NEA, 1976. 92p.
(Grandes Figures Africaines).

Presents a biography of Bokar Biro, whose place in Guinean history has been largely
ignored, despite his role in the late 19th century as a powerful ruler in the Fouta
Djallon who resisted the colonizing advances of the French. He consolidated power
over the region, which had been going through a period of great political and social
turmoil, while the other leaders fought with each other for control.

86 **Alfa Yaya, roi du Labé.** (Alfa Yaya, king of Labé.)
Thierno Diallo.   Paris: ABC; Dakar, Abidjan: NEA, 1976. 89p.
bibliog. (Grandes Figures Africaines).

An account of the life of Alfa Yaya, a king of Labé in the Fouta Djallon, who became
active in the French colonial administration. He was born in 1850 or 1855, and
reigned from 1892 to 1905. However, when he realized that he could not use the
French to fulfill his own ambitions he turned against them and was deported to
Dahomey in 1905. He returned to Guinea in 1910, but was then sent to Mauritania,
where he died in 1912. After independence Alfa Yaya's memory was resurrected and
he was hailed as a hero for his stand against the French.

87 **Cheikh Fanta Madi Cherif, grand marabout de Haut-Guinée.** (Sheik
Fanta Madi Cherif, grand marabout of Upper Guinea.)
Djiba Diané.   *Islam et Sociétés au Sud du Sahara*, no. 2 (1988),
p. 107-13.

A biography of Sheik Fanta Madi Cherif (c.1873-1955), son-in-law of the Islamic
leader Samori Touré, and an influential religious leader at Kankan.

88 **Sékou Touré: le héros et le tyran.** (Sekou Touré: the hero and the tyrant.)
Ibrahima Baba Kaké. Paris: Jeune Afrique, 1987. 254p. bibliog. (Jeune Afrique Livres, no. 3).

This account of Sekou Touré's life looks at the two sides of his political career: the revolutionary who dared to say 'Non' to de Gaulle and claim independence from France with his great ideals; and the paranoid dictator who imagined plots against him, disposing mercilessly of any opposition. Sixteen pages of black-and-white photographs are included under the title 'Séducteur et despote' (Seducer and despot), which illustrate these two sides to the President.

89 **Diallo Telli: le tragique destin d'un grand Africain.** (Diallo Telli: the tragic destiny of a great African.)
André Lewin. Paris: Jeune Afrique, 1990. 225p. (Jeune Afrique Livres, no. 14).

A biography of Diallo Telli, a Fula, who became minister of justice in Sekou Touré's government, but was accused of organizing a plot to overthrow the President in 1976, and eventually died of starvation in Boiro prison camp in 1977. He had an outstanding administrative career in colonial Africa, becoming the first secretary general of the Organisation of African Unity before returning to Guinea after independence as one of Sekou Touré's principal ministers. He was ultimately a victim of the dictator's paranoia. This detailed account is illustrated with black-and-white photographs.

90 **A royal African.**
Prince Modupe. New York: Praeger, 1969. 185p.

Despite the rather patronizing foreword by an American Professor of Anthropology, this is an enlightening account of the childhood of a man born in a village in Guinea to a Soussou royal family. He describes the way of life and the tribal rituals, including initiation ceremonies and the rituals of the Bondo Bush secret societies. The later parts of the book are concerned with the author's move to Sierra Leone, and eventually to America to study in 1922.

91 **Notes sur Alfa Oumar Rafihou de Dara-Labé, environ 1800-1885.** (Notes on Alfa Oumar Rafihou of Dara-Labé, c.1800-85.)
Bernard Salvaing. *Islam et Sociétés au Sud du Sahara*, no. 3 (1989), p. 186-93.

A short biography of an Islamic leader and member of the ruling family of Labé. The Islamic rulers were very influential at the end of the 19th century as they were the chief resistors of the advance of French colonization.

The reds and the blacks: a personal adventure.
See item no. 61.

Camp Boiro: sinistre geôle de Sékou Touré. (Camp Boiro: Sekou Touré's sinister jail.)
See item no. 62.

La mort de Diallo Telli: premier secrétaire général de l'O.A.U. (The death of Diallo Telli: first secretary general of the O.A.U.)
See item no. 66.

First American ambassador to Guinea.
See item no. 73.

Sékou Touré.
See item no. 79.

Guinée: unique survivant du 'Complot Kaman-Fodeba'. (Guinea: sole survivor of the 'Kaman-Fodeba plot'.)
See item no. 83.

The African child.
See item no. 190.

A dream of Africa.
See item no. 191.

Camara Laye: a bio-bibliography.
See item no. 197.

Population

92 **Les Guinéens de l'extérieur: rentrer au pays?** (Guineans abroad:
return to the motherland?)
Amadou Oury Bah, Bintou Keita, Benoit Lootvoet. *Politique
Africaine*, no. 36 (December 1989), p. 22-37.
When Sekou Touré died, one-third of Guineans were in exile. This article, which is
part of a complete journal issue devoted to Guinea after Sekou Touré, examines the
Guinean diaspora and the situation of those who have returned home. Many returned
exiles have found it difficult to reintegrate themselves, and have been unable to
organize themselves into effective political groups.

93 **Recensement général de la population et de l'habitat, fevrier 1983:
analyse des résultats définitifs.** (General census of population and
living conditions, February 1983: analysis of final results.)
Ministère du Plan et de la Coopération Internationale, Bureau National
du Recensement.   Conakry: Ministère du Plan et de la Coopération
Internationale, 1989. 172p.
Presents an analysis of the 1983 census results, broken down into: spatial distribution;
structure by sex and age; religion; marital status; literacy and education levels; death
rates; birth rates and fertility; migration; and living conditions. The total population
was approximately 4.5 million. A later census taken in 1992 estimated the population
at 5.6 million, although this is thought to be an underestimate. The increase is due to a
large number of refugees entering the country from Sierra Leone and Liberia, where
there are ongoing conflicts.

94 **United Nations inter-agency appeal for new refugee outflows and populations affected by the humanitarian situation in Sierra Leone: March-December 1995.**
United Nations, Department of Humanitarian Affairs. New York; Geneva: United Nations, 1995. 26p.

The civil war which has been fought in Sierra Leone since 1991 has led to large numbers of refugees fleeing into Guinea. At the end of 1995 it was estimated that 200,000 Sierra Leonean refugees had sought asylum in Forecariah in Guinea Forestière. The United Nations High Commission for Regugees (UNHCR) and other aid organizations are attempting to provide emergency relief to these people. This paper provides brief descriptions, including financial summaries, of the projects undertaken in Sierra Leone and Guinea.

La genèse du peuplement de Conakry. (Conakry's population in the early days.)
See item no. 48.

Sierra Leoneans in Guinea: an introduction.
See item no. 49.

Ethnic Groups

95 Aristocrats facing change: the Fulbe in Guinea, Nigeria and Cameroon.
Victor Azarya.   Chicago: University of Chicago Press, 1978. 293p.
The Fulbe are also known as the Fula, Fulani and Peul. They regard themselves as aristocrats, and although they were originally nomadic pastoralists, many have now settled in a widespread area of West Africa. This book studies the Fula society of the Fouta Djallon, as well as communities in Nigeria and Cameroon. It covers the history of the Fula people, looking at the pre-colonial period, examining the impacts of colonialism, and finally assessing their status in the independent states which had emerged.

96 Serfs, peasants, and socialists: a former serf village in the Republic of Guinea.
William Derman, with the assistance of Louise Derman.   Berkeley, California: University of California Press, 1973. 282p. map. bibliog.
This looks at the Fula of the Fouta Djallon plateau area and analyses the transformation of their society during the pre-colonial, colonial and post-colonial periods. The study concentrates on the sedentary Fula in the village of Hollaande and examines the changing relationships between the ruling Fula and the people who originally served them as serfs.

97 The sacred forest: the fetishist and magic rites of the Toma.
Pierre-Dominique Gaisseau, translated by Alan Ross.   London: Weidenfeld & Nicolson, 1954. 199p.
This is a very detailed and graphic account of the experiences of four Frenchmen living with the Toma, a minority ethnic group who live in the forested areas straddling the Liberia border in the south-east of Guinea. The men spent some time gaining the trust and acceptance of the Toma, and took part in many of the secret initiation ceremonies and rituals, held in sacred areas in the forest, which are described in great detail. There are thirty-two black-and-white photographs.

98 **Peuples de la fôret de Guinée.** (Peoples of the forest of Guinea.)
   Jacques Germain.   Paris: Académie des Sciences d'Outre-Mer, 1984.
   381p. maps. bibliog.
Describes the various ethnic groups of the forest regions of Upper Guinea. The
account looks at the history of the area and of the people, their social and political
organization and religious ceremonies, as well as their arts and crafts. There are fold-
out maps and black-and-white photographs throughout the text.

99 **Contes Kono: traditions populaires de la forêt guinéenne.** (Kono
   stories: popular traditions of the Guinea forest.)
   B. Holas.   Paris: G. P. Maisonneuve et Larose, 1975. 343p.
A collection of popular stories from the Nzérékoré region, divided into broad subjects:
ancient tales, people and customs, fables, and riddles, accompanied by a number of
explanatory drawings. The author has written widely on Guinean folklore and his
other works include *Les masques Kono, leur rôle dans la vie religieuse et politique,
Haute Guinée française* (Kono masks, their role in religious and political life, Upper
Guinea) (Paris: Geuthner, 1952), as well as a number of journal articles.

100 **Les Coniagui et les Bassari (Guinée française).** (The Coniagui and
   the Bassari.)
   Monique de Lestrange.   Paris: Presses Universitaires de France, 1955.
   86p. map. bibliog. (Monographies Ethnologiques Africaines).
Describes the Coniagui (also known as the Konagi) and the Bassari minority ethnic
groups, who live in the north of the country on the Fouta Djallon and the borders of
Senegal and Guinea-Bissau. Both groups are among the oldest inhabitants of Guinea
and have retained their language, religions and customs, in spite of competition from
the dominant Malinké and Fula groups. See also *Coniagui women* by Monique
Gessain (q.v.).

101 **Les gens du riz: Kissi de haute-guinée française.** (The rice people:
   the Kissi of Upper Guinea.)
   Denise Paulme.   Paris: Librairie Plon, 1954. 233p. (Recherches en
   Sciences Humaines, no. 4).
This is a classic study of the Kissi and their way of life, including information on
customs, rituals, food production, social structure and magic, and illustrated by
photographs throughout the text. A second edition was published in 1970. The author
has written numerous articles on the Kissi and the Baga, and also a book on the Kissi
language: *Documents sur la langue Kissi: lexique et textes* (Documents on the Kissi
language: vocabulary and texts) (Dakar: Université de Dakar, 1964).

102 **Fabulous ancestors: stone carvings from Sierra Leone and Guinea.**
   Aldo Tagliaferri, Arno Hammacher.   Milan, Italy: Edizioni il Polifilio,
   1974. 195p. 2 maps. bibliog.
The Kissi in Guinea and the Mende in Sierra Leone find these stone carvings buried in
the ground and claim that they represent their ancestors. The carvings, made of steatite
or soapstone, are usually between ten and twenty centimetres high and are known as
nomoli or *pomdo*. The book has an introductory section followed by eighty black-and-

white plates of various figures, accompanied by notes on where they were found and where they are located now.

'Two hippos cannot live in one river.' Zo Musa, Foningama, and the founding of Musadu in the oral traditions of the Konyaka.
See item no. 37.

La genèse du peuplement de Conakry. (Conakry's population in the early days.)
See item no. 48.

A royal African.
See item no. 90.

La langue Guerzé – grammaire Guerzé. (Guerzé language – Guerzé grammar.)
See item no. 104.

L'Islam en Guinée: Fouta-Diallon. (Islam in Guinea: Fouta Djallon.)
See item no. 111.

Coniagui women.
See item no. 117.

Le foncier en Guinée. (Land tenure in Guinea.)
See item no. 168.

Salvage anthropology: the redesign of a rural development project in Guinea.
See item no. 169.

Whose social forestry and why? People, trees and managed continuity in Guinea's forest-savanna mosaic.
See item no. 182.

Contes et récits peuls du Fouta Djalon. (Fula stories and narratives from the Fouta Djallon.)
See item no. 203.

La femme, la vache, la foi: écrivains et poètes du Foûta Djalon. (The woman, the cow, the faith: writers and poets of the Fouta Djallon.)
See item no. 204.

Poèmes peuls du Fouta Djallon. (Fula poems from the Fouta Djallon.)
See item no. 205.

Musique Malinké: Guinée. Record review.
See item no. 209.

Les Kissi: une société noire et ses instruments de musique. (The Kissi: a black society and their musical instruments.)
See item no. 211.

Toward a Kpelle conceptualization of music performance.
See item no. 212.

Languages

103 Manuel pratique de langue Peulh. (Practical manual of the Fula language.)
L. Arensdorff. Paris: Librairie Paul Geuthner, 1913. 424p. map.
This study of the Fula (Peulh) language was undertaken primarily in Guinea, although the mainly nomadic people known as Fula (also Peul, Fulani, Fulbe) inhabit a wide area of West Africa. An introductory chapter covers the origins, physique and habitat of the Fula, while following sections cover morphology, syntax, prosody, idioms and proverbs in Fula. Words are written in arabic script, and translations are provided into roman type and French.

104 La langue Guerzé – grammaire Guerzé. (Guerzé language – Guerzé grammar.)
R. P. J. Casthelain, R. P. P. Lassort. Dakar: Institut Français d'Afrique Noire, 1952. 422p. (Mémoires IFAN, no. 20).
The Guerzé are also known as the Kpelle and live in the Nzérékoré area of Guinea. This very comprehensive book is divided into two parts, each by a different author: the first part examines the syntax of the language and has a Guerzé-French dictionary of nearly 200 pages; and the second part is a grammar of the language.

105 English-Fula dictionary (Fulfulde, Pulaar, Fulani): a multidialectal approach.
Paul P. De Wolf. Berlin: Dietrich Reimer Verlag, 1995. 3 vols.
bibliog.
The Fula (Peul, Fulani) live in a wide area of West Africa, including Guinea. Compiled over fifteen years, this huge work in three large volumes provides as many Fula dialect equivalents for English words as possible. There is an introductory section of over 100 pages on the grammar of the language, and each alphabetical section of the dictionary is numbered separately. This is an invaluable dictionary for anyone wishing to learn the language.

106 **Structure du badiaranke de Guinée et du Sénégal: phonologie, syntaxe.** (Linguistic analysis of Guinean and Senegalese Badiaranke: phonemics and syntax.)
Gisèle Ducos. Paris: Société pour l'Étude des Langues Africaines, 1971. 294p.

The Badiaranke live in the northern part of Guinea, spreading into Senegal and Guinea-Bissau. The language, spoken by about 5,500 people, is classified as a member of the Tende group, along with Bassari and Coniagui. This book explains the phonemic system and goes on to provide a grammatical analysis of the language.

107 **Dictionnaire peul-français.** (Fula-French dictionary.)
Henri Gaden. Dakar: Institut Fondamental d'Afrique Noire, 1969. , 120p. (Catalogues et Documents, no. 22).

A reproduction of the original work by the author, dated 1914, supplemented by the work of a team of researchers from the Fouta Djallon and the Fouta Toro of Senegal, indicating particular Fula (Peul) dialect words from these areas. Many words are also illustrated with proverbs.

108 **Proverbes et maximes Peuls et Toucouleurs traduits, expliqués et annotés.** (Proverbs and maxims of the Fula and Toucouleurs translated, explained and annotated.)
Henri Gaden. Paris: Institut d'Ethnologie, 1931. 368p.

Comprises proverbs from the Fouta Djallon and the Fouta Toro of Senegal, with an introduction on Fula (Peul) grammar. The proverbs are divided into categories such as the family, power, good and bad, with French translations and notes on usage.

109 **Étude descriptive de la langue Susu.** (Descriptive study of the Soussou language.)
Maurice Houis. Dakar: Institut Français d'Afrique Noire, 1963. 183p. bibliog. (Mémoires IFAN, no. 67).

Covers the phonology and grammar of the Soussou language in great detail. A dictionary of the Soussou language is published as *Grammaire et dictionnaire français-soussou et soussou-français* (A French-Soussou/Soussou-French grammar and dictionary) by R. P. Lacan (Bordeaux: Saint-Esprit, 1942).

Religion

110 **Révolte, pouvoir, religion: les Hubbu de Futa-Jalon (Guinée).**
(Revolt, power, religion: the Hubbu of Fouta Djallon [Guinea].)
Roger Botte. *Journal of African History*, vol. 29, no. 3 (1988),
p. 391-413.
Examines the power struggles during the mid-19th century between the Islamic rulers
of the Fouta Djallon and the Hubbu movement, a religious fraternity, founded in 1845
by Alfa Mamadu Dyuhe. The Fouta state, which had been founded by an Islamic
revolution in the 18th century, lost the support of its Fula founders due to the
oppression of much of the population. The Fula and Malinké were particularly
responsive to Alfa Mamadu's preachings, and at the height of its success the Hubbu
took possession of the Fouta state capital of Timbo. However, after Alfa Mamadu's
death in 1854 the members failed to carry through the revolution and turned to
banditry. This article is summarized in English.

111 **L'Islam en Guinée: Fouta-Diallon.** (Islam in Guinea: Fouta Djallon.)
Paul Marty. Paris: Leroux, 1921. 588p. maps. bibliog.
An extremely detailed and important account of the Islamization of the Fouta Djallon.
The author discusses the power of the almami and the influence of Islam on the
culture, education, laws and social customs of the various tribal groups.

112 **Tcherno Aliou, the Wali of Goumba: Islam, colonialism and the
rural factor in Futa Jallon, 1867-1912.**
L. Sanneh. *Asian and African Studies*, vol. 20, no. 1 (1986), p. 73-
102.
Tcherno Aliou was born c.1828 and settled in the village of Goumba in 1867, a time
of social and political unrest, when the French were attempting to penetrate the Fouta
Djallon, but also a time when the old religious élite was being superseded by the new
Islamic leadership, including Tcherno Aliou. The author argues that it was the rural
factor which led to religious militancy.

113 **Touba in Guinea: holy place of Islam.**
Jean Suret-Canale.   In: *African perspectives.*   Edited by Christopher
Allen, R. W. Johnson.   Cambridge, England: Cambridge University
Press, 1970, p. 53-81.

Although situated in the north-west of the Fouta Djallon, in the heart of Fula country,
Touba is populated by Diakhanké people. It was founded in 1823-24 by Al Hadj
Salimou, known as Karamoko-ba, who was a Muslim teacher. He built a mosque at
Touba, where he had finally settled after much wandering, and his reputation was such
that Muslims still go there on pilgrimage and for religious instruction. This article
details the founding of the town and various events in its history, including incidents
in 1908 and 1911 caused by disagreements among the Diakhanké.

Mutations sociales en Guinée. (Social changes in Guinea.)
See item no. 116.

Le foncier en Guinée. (Land tenure in Guinea.)
See item no. 168.

Social Conditions

114 **Erotisme africain: le comportement sexuel des adolescents guinéens.** (African eroticism: sexual behaviour of Guinean adolescents.)
Pierre Hanry. Paris: Payot, 1970. 201p. bibliog.
The three parts of this book cover adolescents and their families, including: initiation and circumcision ceremonies; the sexual life of boys and girls; and the sexual economy, including the need for better sex education.

115 **Classes et stratifications sociales en Afrique: le cas guinéen.** (Social classes and stratifications in Africa: the Guinean case.)
Claude Rivière. Paris: Presses Universitaires de France, 1978. 296p. bibliog. (Publications de la Sorbonne, N. S. Recherches, no. 24).
Looks at the structure of Guinean society within the socialist régime of Sekou Touré. Traditional society was very hierarchical and patriarchal, a structure upon which Touré built his socialism. The book is divided into sections on: the bourgeoisie who formed the élites of society; the working classes; and the peasants, who themselves were divided into the producers and the controllers of production. The author has written widely on Guinean social issues, including a thesis: *Dynamique de la stratification sociale en Guinée* (Dynamics of social stratification in Guinea) (Paris: Université de Paris V, 1975), and *Mutations sociales en Guinée* (q.v.).

116 **Mutations sociales en Guinée.** (Social changes in Guinea.)
Claude Rivière. Paris: Rivière, 1971. 418p.
Looks at the social changes that took place in Guinea as a result of the declaration of independence and the influence of Sekou Touré, who strove to modernize traditional customs. There are chapters on ethnic integration, the status of women, political mobilization of the young, the demystification of fetishism, Islamization and the retreat of Catholicism.

L'ajustement au quotidien. (Day to day adjustment.)
See item no. 149.

Women

117 **Coniagui women.**
Monique Gessain. In: *Women of tropical Africa.* Edited by Denise
Paulme. London: Routledge & Kegan Paul, 1963, p. 17-46.
The book is a translation by H. M. Wright of *Femmes d'Afrique noir* (Paris: Mouton,
1960). This particular chapter is a study of the role of women in Coniagui and Bassari
society in Guinea. It examines the kinship links and relationships with men, the
position of women through childhood, adolescence, marriage and motherhood, and
includes several passages from autobiographical accounts of Coniagui people.

118 **Women literacy in Guinea.**
Diamilatou Sow. *African Association for Literacy and Adult
Education Journal*, vol. 6, no. 1 (1992), p. 6-14.
The illiteracy rate in Guinea is seventy-five per cent, and women constitute eighty-six
per cent of this figure. In 1985 the notion of functional literacy was developed, which
relates literacy to community development. The National Literacy Service in Guinea
has therefore organized women's programmes in order to help them improve their
living conditions.

119 **Guinea: gender issues.**
World Bank, Africa Region, Women in Development Team.
[Washington, DC]: World Bank, 1993. [11p.]. (Information Sheet,
no. 1.15).
Presents a brief survey of the legal position of women within the constitution, and
women's status within the strategic sectors of education, health, agriculture,
employment and credit. It includes tables of key socio-economic indicators for the
years 1970 to 1990.

Health and Welfare

120 **Determinants of vaccination in an urban population in Conakry, Guinea.**
F. T. Cutts, S. Diallo, E. R. Zell, P. Rhodes. *International Journal of Epidemiology*, vol. 20, no. 4 (1991), p. 1,099-106.

The Expanded Program on Immunization (EPI) was begun in 1974 in order to achieve global immunization against polio and diptheria/pertussis/tetanus. It was set up in Conakry in 1979. This paper examines the results of a survey of vaccination in Conakry and reports on the impact of missed vaccination opportunities. It also assesses the interaction between the mother's educational level and other determinants of vaccination, and presents multivariate analysis of the results of sample surveys. The conclusion reached is that vaccination coverage could be increased by: improving health services, following the vaccination schedule correctly and reducing waiting times.

121 **Stratégie de coopération de l'UNICEF dans le domaine de la santé publique en Guinée.** (Cooperative strategy of UNICEF in the public health area in Guinea.)
Alpha Telly Diallo. Conakry: UNICEF, 1990. 76p. bibliog.
(Document de Travail, ASMEG/UNICEF/02).

UNICEF (United Nations Children's Fund) has been present in Guinea since 1979, and opened a national office there in 1985. It has cooperated with various government departments in developing programmes to improve the situation of women and children. On average, women have their first child between the ages of fourteen and twenty, and often have no access to maternity services, health care, family planning, or even clean drinking water. Infant and maternal mortality rates are high, but could be reduced by the introduction of basic infrastructural services.

122 **The impact of permanent disability on rural households: river blindness in Guinea.**
Timothy Evans. *IDS Bulletin*, vol. 20, no. 2 (1989), p. 41-48.

This article considers the impact of blindness on small households in areas of highly endemic river blindness (onchocerciasis). Although there has been much research on the disease and its control, previously there has been little study of the economic consequences of river blindness, whose preferred victims are males in the prime of their working lives.

123 **Private participation in the delivery of Guinea's water supply services.**
Thelma A. Triche. Washington, DC: World Bank, Infrastructure and Urban Development Department, 1990. 30p. (Policy, Research and External Affairs Working Papers, WPS 477).

Examines an urban water supply project which became effective in 1989. The World Bank helped to finance the scheme whereby a state enterprise, the Société Nationale des Eaux de Guinée (SONEG), owns the urban water supply facilities, which are operated as a commercial enterprise by the Société d'Exploitation des Eaux de Guinée (SEEG). Before 1989 Guinea had one of the least developed water supplies in West Africa, despite adequate natural water resources.

Politics and
Administration

124 **Quadrillage politique et administratif des militaires.** (Political and administrative control of the military.)
Bernard Charles. *Politique Africaine*, no. 36 (December 1989), p. 9-21.

This article, which is part of a complete journal issue on Guinea after Sekou Touré, examines how the military leaders of the Comité militaire de redressement national (CMRN) have reorganized the administrative system without, however, substituting a Soussou state for a Malinké state.

125 **Guinea.**
L. Gray Cowan. In: *African one-party states.* Edited by Gwendolen M. Carter. Ithaca, New York: Cornell University Press, 1962, p. 149-236. map. bibliog.

After an introductory section on Guinea's historical background and French colonial rule, this chapter, written not long after independence, examines the rise of the nationalist movement and the struggle for independence. It also discusses the Parti démocratique de Guinée (PDG) and its part in the development of Guinean society. It gives a detailed account of the early years of the PDG and of Sekou Touré's role in it.

126 **Guinée: l'an I de la reconstruction.** (Guinea: the first year of reconstruction.)
Sory Diallo. *Géopolitique Africaine*, [no. 1] (March 1986), p. 153-69.

Assesses Lansana Conté's first year of leadership, following his seizure of power in 1984. There were substantial administrative reforms and liberalizations as the country looked forward optimistically to a return to democracy and freedom of human rights, after the atrocities of Sekou Touré.

127 **Guinea's 'non-capitalist' way.**
J. N. Hazard. *Columbia Journal of Transnational Law*, vol. 5, no. 2 (1966), p. 231-62.
This is part of a comparison between African socialist law and Marxian socialist law. It includes information on Sekou Touré's views, sections on the country's administration, as well as civil and criminal law under Touré's 'non-capitalist' way.

128 **Guinea: united against the world.**
Kenneth Ingham. In: *Politics in modern Africa: the uneven tribal dimension.* London: Routledge, 1990, p. 135-53.
Discusses Sekou Touré's period of office and his desire to govern the people of Guinea as a whole, regardless of their tribal origins. He felt that all Guineans should be united against French domination. However, many of the better educated and skilled Guineans fled the country, leaving a lack of trained personnel to implement the development plans. Following Sekou Touré's death in 1984, little changed as the influences of Touré's years in office were deeply entrenched. The insistence upon self-reliance and rejection of foreign assistance led to continuing economic problems, and the continued exile of many Guineans.

129 **The Parti démocratique de Guinée and the Mamou 'deviation'.**
R. W. Johnson. In: *African Perspectives.* Edited by Christopher Allen, R. W. Johnson. Cambridge, England: Cambridge University Press, 1970, p. 347-69.
A particularly militant section of the PDG developed in the early 1950s at Mamou, a region in the Fouta Djallon, and this paper looks at the reasons for its development. There was friction between the Mamou and Conakry factions, but after the 1957 elections Sekou Touré's leadership triumphed and the radical Mamou 'deviation' was ousted.

130 **National integration: contrasting ideologies in Guinea.**
Peter M. Slowe. In: *Third World regional development: a reappraisal.* Edited by David Simon. London: Paul Chapman, 1990, p. 39-55.
This chapter contrasts the political ideologies of Sekou Touré and Lansana Conté, and compares the effects each had on the national integration of a state with an ethnically diverse population. To Touré, national and class integration was important in order to create a national identity. In contrast, Conté has pursued economic development policies within the international capitalist economy. The author regards this combination of policies as a cause for optimism for the future growth of the country.

The political thought of Sékou Touré.
See item no. 60.

Internal capacity and overload in Guinea and Niger.
See item no. 146.

Foreign Relations

131 **The Mano River Union: an experiment in economic integration.**
Augustus F. Caine. *Liberian Studies Journal*, vol. 13, no. 1 (1988), p. 6-41.

The Mano River Union was created in 1973 as a customs union between Liberia and Sierra Leone. Guinea joined in October 1980. This paper outlines the Union's objectives and some of its achievements. The main objective was to accelerate economic growth, social progress and cultural achievement in the member states by liberalizing trade and opening up markets to each other. However, despite some early optimism, the hoped-for results were never realized, and by the end of the 1980s the Union collapsed, partly due to the unfavourable international economic situation of the time.

132 **La Guinée sans la France.** (Guinea without France.)
Sylvain Soriba Camara. [Paris]: Fondation Nationale des Sciences Politiques, 1976. 299p. bibliog. (Travaux et Recherches de Science Politique, no. 44).

Discusses the events leading up to the 1958 referendum, in which Guinea overwhelmingly rejected France's invitation to membership of a French African community, and the consequent breakdown in relations between the two countries. It also deals with the effects on Guinea's relations with the other French African states.

133 **Changing relations among Guinea, the Ivory Coast, and Mali.**
Victor D. Du Bois. *American Universities Field Staff (AUFS) Reports: West Africa Series*, vol. 5, no. 4 (1962), p. 39-52.

Reports on the Rassemblement démocratique africaine (RDA), founded in 1946, which had all but ceased with the independence of the French West African countries. Views had become polarized between Sekou Touré, with his radical anti-colonial views, and President Félix Houphouët-Boigny of the Ivory Coast who was in favour of a Franco-African community. Relations between Guinea, the Ivory Coast and Mali became tense, but by 1962 they were moving together again and official visits were being undertaken.

134 **Livre blanc sur le prétendu conflit frontalier entre la République de Guinée-Bissao et la République Populaire Révolutionnaire de Guinée.** (Report on the alleged border dispute between Guinea-Bissau and the Popular Revolutionary Republic of Guinea.)
Conakry: Parti-Etat de Guinée, 1980. 45p.

This official publication on the border dispute with Guinea-Bissau includes a copy of the original Convention of 1886 between France and Portugal, which set the boundaries of their West African territories.

135 **Guinea: a challenge to American foreign policy.**
Thomas Patrick Melady. In: *An evaluation of the United States' position in Guinea, Liberia and Ghana.* Pittsburgh, Pennsylvania: Duquesne University Press, 1960, p. 3-6.

A rather paranoid article about 'red penetration' in Guinea in the early years of Sekou Touré's government following French withdrawal. The Americans were terrified of the communists gaining control in Africa, and the American author of this piece recommends that America try to neutralize the Soviet beach-head in Guinea.

136 **The international policy of the Democratic Party of Guinea.**
Ahmed Sekou Touré. [Conakry]: S.O.P. Press, [1963]. 241p.

Collected here are speeches by Sekou Touré given at various international conferences and meetings, including several sessions of the United Nations. The selection includes a speech given in 1961 on the Guinean position regarding the war in Algeria, and an address on the Ghana-Guinea-Mali Union, given at a meeting of the three heads of state in 1960.

Le 'Non' de la Guinée à de Gaulle. (Guinea's 'No' to de Gaulle.)
See item no. 51.

The reds and the blacks: a personal adventure.
See item no. 61.

First American ambassador to Guinea.
See item no. 73.

Economy

137 **Policy failure and the limits of rapid reform: lessons from Guinea.**
Jehan Arulpragrasam, David E. Sahn.   In: *Adjusting to policy failure
in African economies*.   Edited by David E. Sahn.   Ithaca, New York:
Cornell University Press, 1994, p. 53-95.
The economic crisis in Guinea in the 1980s was not due to external factors such as
drought or war, as has been the case in other African countries, but due to internal
economic policy failure. This paper presents a study of the way in which policy failure
in the twenty-five years after independence led to economic crisis, and how
subsequent policy reform has addressed the problems. The speed of reform under
Lansana Conté's Second Republic was remarkable, but the paper shows that growth
requires more than adjustment policies – the infrastructure of transport systems, health
and education also need to be developed.

138 **Guinée, deuxième gouvernement de la deuxième République, an
deux.** (Guinea, second government of the Second Republic, second
year.)
Guy Caire.   *Mondes en Développement*, vol. 16, no. 62-63 (1988),
p. 15-33.
Examines the consequences of the new economic policies initiated by Lansana Conté
in 1985 as part of the drastic economic restructuring following Sekou Touré's death.

139 **Guinea's economic performance under structural adjustment:
importance of mining and agriculture.**
Bonnie Campbell, Jennifer Clapp.   *Journal of Modern African
Studies*, vol. 33, no. 3 (1995), p. 425-49.
Since it adopted a structural adjustment programme in late 1985, sponsored by the
World Bank and the International Monetary Fund, Guinea's economic performance
has not met expectations. This paper argues that external factors have been equally
important as internal policy failings in explaining this. Both mining and agriculture
are key sectors in Guinea's economy, but fluctuations in the world prices of

aluminium and the main crops of rice and coffee have played a critical role in Guinea's economic difficulties.

140 **Country presentation: Guinea.**
Geneva: United Nations, 1990. 49p. (UNCLDC II/CP.41).

This presentation by the government of Guinea to the United Nations Conference on the Least Developed Countries held in Paris from 3 to 14 September 1990, presents a diagnosis of Guinea's situation in the economic, financial and social spheres, and examines the prospects for the year 2000. The main objectives are to liberalize the country's economy in order to enable the people to take advantage of Guinea's wealth of natural resources. To achieve this the government aims to diversify the economy and encourage the development of the private sector.

141 **Reorganization of the Guinean economy: the attempts to remove the economic vestiges of colonialism.**
Victor Du Bois. *American Universities Field Staff (AUFS) Reports: West Africa Series*, vol. 6, no. 1 (1963), p. 1-22.

With independence in 1958 and the withdrawal of the French, the Guinean economy was drastically restructured by Sekou Touré. This paper analyses these changes and discusses *investissement humain*, 'human investment', a programme of using unpaid volunteer labour for the construction of public-works projects in order to hasten economic development.

142 **Guinea, Sierra Leone, Liberia: country profile.**
Economist Intelligence Unit. London: Economist Intelligence Unit, 1993- . annual.

A very useful publication which provides up-to-date information on the political and economic situation in the country. It is divided into sections covering: political background; population and society; currency; the economy; national accounts; employment; wages and prices; agriculture, forestry and fishing; mining; energy; manufacturing; construction; commerce and tourism; transport and communications; finance; foreign trade; external payments and debt; and exchange, trade and investment regulations. This grouping of countries supersedes the Unit's previous grouping of *Guinea, Mali, Mauritania: country profile.*

143 **Guinea, Sierra Leone, Liberia: country report.**
Economist Intelligence Unit. London: Economist Intelligence Unit, 1993- . quarterly.

Complementary to the Unit's annual *Country profile* (q.v.), this quarterly report presents up-to-date information on the political and economic structure of Guinea, with tables of economic indicators and trade figures. It presents a review of recent events and gives a political and economic outlook for up to two years. It supersedes the Unit's *Guinea, Mali, Mauritania: country report.*

144 **Guinée 1994: au-delà de Conakry.** (Guinea 1994: beyond Conakry.)
Michel Gaud. *Afrique Contemporaine*, no. 173 (1995), p. 3-13.

It is the situation in Conakry which projects the image to the world of Guinea as a poor nation. But, this paper argues that the situation in the rural areas gives rise to optimism, as economic progress is being made, especially in agriculture, which could well accelerate in a stable political climate.

145 **Les institutions de Bretton Woods en république de Guinée.**
(Bretton Woods institutions in the Republic of Guinea.)
L. Gilles. *Politique Africaine*, no. 36 (December 1989), p. 71-83.

This article is from a journal issue entirely devoted to Guinea after Sekou Touré. The author argues that studies of economic adjustment programmes in some African countries often lead to hasty and negative judgements that do not reflect the real efforts made by these countries. In the case of Guinea, adjustment has been dictated by experts in Washington, and Guinea itself has been unable to negotiate the terms.

146 **Internal capacity and overload in Guinea and Niger.**
N. Lynn Graybeal, Louis A. Picard. *Journal of Modern African Studies*, vol. 29, no. 2 (1991), p. 275-300.

Examines the effects of structural adjustment programmes on the political systems of Guinea and Niger. Following Sekou Touré's death in 1984 the military government sought a loan from the International Monetary Fund (IMF), who imposed a number of strict reforms, including the demand for a large reduction in the public sector. This paper looks at the resistance to this and argues that the IMF has been insensitive to the historical basis of the administration systems and the difficulties encountered in implementing reforms.

147 **Rapport Economique et Social.** (Economic and Social Report.)
Ministère du Plan et des Finances, Direction Nationale du Plan et du Développement Economique. Conakry: Ministère du Plan et des Finances, 1990- . annual.

Presents economic and social indicators for the previous year, and prospects for the following year. In 1992 the Direction Nationale du Plan et du Développement Economique changed its name to Direction Nationale du Plan et de l'Economie.

148 **Tableau de Bord de l'Economie Guinéenne.** (Economic Indicators of Guinea.)
Ministère du Plan et des Finances, Direction Nationale du Plan et du Développement Economique. Conakry: Ministère du Plan et des Finances, 1989- . quarterly.

A regular summary of various economic indicators such as inflation, salaries, exports, government resources, credit, and Guinea's place in the world economy.

149 **L'ajustement au quotidien.** (Day to day adjustment.)
Jacques Schwartz. *Politique Africaine*, no. 36 (December 1989), p. 84-96.

By dismantling the former administrative system, the military government has upset the 'food protectorate' enjoyed by public service workers. The resulting rise in speculation has led to a price explosion and has deepened social inequalities in Conakry, where many households are barely surviving.

150 **Spécial Guinée.** (Guinea special.)
Marchés Tropicaux et Méditerranéens, no. 2,489 (July 1993),
p. 1,893-916.

The special section on Guinea in this journal is divided into sections covering: economic development; money and banking; agriculture; mining; commerce and industry; transport; electricity; and tourism.

151 **Réajuster l'économie: premier bilan des réformes.** (Readjusting the
economy: first results of the reforms.)
Yves Topol. *Politique Africaine*, no. 36 (December 1989), p. 56-70.

This article, from a journal issue entirely devoted to Guinea after Sekou Touré, looks at the results of the economic adjustment policies imposed by the International Monetary Fund and the World Bank in 1985. These liberal reforms were aimed at the public sector, but the move towards Westernization, the gaps in the rhythm of the reforms and the persistence of corruption have engendered political tensions, and the problems of development have not been solved.

152 **Guinea: the significance of the coup of April 1984 and economic
issues.**
Aguibou Y. Yansané. *World Development*, vol. 18, no. 9 (1990),
p. 1,231-46.

Sekou Touré's régime had brought about economic stagnation in Guinea. The new military régime that seized power in 1984 has attempted to rebuild the economy, introducing structural adjustment programmes and administrative reforms. This article takes an optimistic view of the economic future under Lansana Conté and the Comité militaire de redressement national (CMRN).

L'intoxication anti-française des trafiquants. (The anti-French poisoning
of traders.)
See item no. 153.

Les hommes d'affaires guinéens. (Guinean businessmen.)
See item no. 154.

**The Popular Revolutionary Republic of Guinea: effective discrimination
against small farmers in a socialist economy.**
See item no. 166.

Trade

153 **L'intoxication anti-française des trafiquants.** (The anti-French poisoning of traders.)
Sory Diallo. *Géopolitique Africaine*, [no. 2] (June 1986), p. 251-62.
Discusses the intervention of various international organizations, such as the World Bank, International Monetary Fund and the United Nations Development Fund, in Guinea's economic reconstruction. It argues that Guinea's trade links have been damaged by the imposition of these economic measures.

154 **Les hommes d'affaires guinéens.** (Guinean businessmen.)
Agnès Lambert. *Cahiers d'Etudes Africaines*, vol. 31, no. 4 (1991), p. 487-508.
An article which examines the way Guinean businessmen have reacted to the liberalization policies since 1984. This study of rice importers in 1990 identifies three groups: 'outside' Guinean businessmen, foreign businesmen, and 'inside' Guinean traders who have never left the country. Having shared out business between themselves, these operators have hindered the process of opening up the country to competition.

Commerce et colonisation en Guinée, 1850-1913. (Commerce and colonization in Guinea, 1850-1913.)
See item no. 47.

The Mano River Union: an experiment in economic integration.
See item no. 131.

Industry

155 Mineral and energy resources and their impact on industrialisation in Guinea.
Ousmane Souaré, Diao Diallo, Alpha Mady Soumah.   In:
Industrialisation, mineral resources and energy in Africa.   Edited by
Smail Khennas.   Dakar: CODESRIA, 1992, p. 127-53.

This chapter attempts to explain the paradox of Guinea's lack of industrial development in contrast with the country's rich endowment of natural resources, particularly bauxite, iron ore and other minerals, as well as great hydroelectric potential. Guinea's case seems to show that however abundant a country's natural resources, this is no guarantee of industrialization.

156 A programme for the development of the fisheries industrial system in the Republic of Guinea.
United Nations Industrial Development Organization, Industrial
Planning Branch.   Vienna: United Nations Industrial Development
Organization, 1989. 56p. (Working Papers in Industrial Planning,
no. 2).

Assesses the status of the fishing sector in Guinea in 1987, and outlines planned development projects. There are no medium or large-scale industrial operations or processing facilities in the Guinean fishing sector.

L'avenir de la Guinée française. (The future of French Guinea.)
See item no. 54.

Spécial Guinée. (Guinea special.)
See item no. 150.

Mineral Resources

157   **Negotiating the bauxite/aluminium sector under narrowing constraints.**
Bonnie K. Campbell.   *Review of African Political Economy*, no. 51 (July 1991), p. 27-49.
Guinea possesses approximately one-third of the world's highest grade bauxite deposits and is the world's leading exporter of this commodity. However, in spite of efforts by the Guinean government to relocate the industry so that bauxite can be processed into alumina in Guinea itself, the aluminium transnationals continue to export raw bauxite. This article summarizes the history of bauxite and alumina production in Guinea, and discusses the debates concerning relocation in the international aluminium industry.

158   **Le secteur de la bauxite en République de Guinée; ajustement structurel et restructuration internationale de l'industrie de l'aluminium.** (The bauxite sector in the Republic of Guinea: structural adjustment and international restructuring of the international aluminium industry.)
Bonnie K. Campbell.   *Revue Tiers Monde*, vol. 34, no. 133 (1993), p. 187-208.
Analyses the importance of the bauxite sector to the Guinean economy, within the structural adjustment policies, and assesses the contribution of the mining sector to public finances and export revenues. The conclusion reached is that the huge potential remains to be fully exploited.

159   **Les bauxites de Guinée.** (Guinean bauxites.)
Jean Charbonneaux.   *Industries et Travaux d'Outre-Mer*, vol. 22, no. 247 (1974), p. 565-70. map.
Bauxite production still dominates the Guinean mining industry, as it did at the time this paper was written. The four main mining sites at Fria, Sangaredi-Boké, Kindia and Dabola-Tougué are described, and there are several black-and-white photographs.

160 **Guinée: potentialités et réalités.** (Guinea: potentialities and realities.)
Sory Diallo. *Géopolitique Africaine*, [no. 3] (Oct. 1986), p. 117-28.
Discusses the negotiations between Guinea and the multinational corporations involved in the exploitation of Guinea's bauxite reserves, concerning the amount of tax paid to the Guinea government. Guinea has never felt the full financial benefit of its natural resources, which have been exported to the benefit of foreign companies.

Guinea and Sierra Leone.
See item no. 19.

Drainage basin evolution in southeast Guinea and the development of diamondiferous placer deposits.
See item no. 20.

Guinea's economic performance under structural adjustment: importance of mining and agriculture.
See item no. 139.

Spécial Guinée. (Guinea special.)
See item no. 150.

Mineral and energy resources and their impact on industrialization in Guinea.
See item no. 155.

Le foncier en Guinée. (Land tenure in Guinea.)
See item no. 168.

Agriculture

161 **La politique agricole, un concept vide? Les effets pervers de l'ouverture libérale.** (Agricultural policy: an empty concept? Perverse effects of liberalization.)
Annie Chéneau-Loquay. *Politique Africaine*, no. 36 (December 1989), p. 38-55.

This article, from a journal issue entirely devoted to Guinea after Sekou Touré, looks at the liberalization of agricultural policies. The effect has been to accentuate the contradictions between the government, funding agencies and rural merchants. There has been a significant rise in food dependence and farmers have suffered a double penalty: they can neither produce more nor increase their prices in the urban markets. A more locally oriented policy, based on the country's tradition of rice production and the regional market, might be more in tune with the real desire for rural development.

162 **Interpreting agricultural performance in Guinea under structural adjustment.**
Jennifer A. Clapp. *Canadian Journal of African Studies*, vol. 27, no. 2 (1993), p. 173-95. bibliog.

Examines the mixed reactions of the agricultural sector to the market reforms introduced under the structural adjustment programme of the mid-1980s. It concludes that the World Bank needs to invest more time and resources at grass roots level if its reforms are to be successful.

163 **Quel avenir pour l'arachide en Haute-Guinée? Les conséquences des interventions sur la production et la commercialisation d'une culture de rente.** (What future for peanuts in Upper Guinea? The consequences of government actions on the production and marketing of a cash crop.)
Anne Gassiat-Sanguinet. *Cahiers d'Outre-Mer*, vol. 46, no. 183 (1993), p. 273-95.

Peanuts continue to be the main cash crop in Upper Guinea. Crop production suffered under the Sekou Touré government, which aimed to establish a steady supply to an oil works. However, the farmers continued to produce the crop for local markets, and it now constitutes the main source of income for villagers. The article examines the marketing chains and price fluctuations of the crop.

164 **Ruined settlements and new gardens: gender and soil-ripening among Kuranko farmers in the forest-savanna transition zone.**
Melissa Leach, James Fairhead. *IDS Bulletin*, vol. 26, no. 1 (1995), p. 24-32.

Examines the changing patterns of gendered resource use in Kuranko 'gardens' in the Kissidougou area. Abandoned villages and habitations are much favoured as farm land, as the soil is more workable and productive after years of use and manuring. This soil ripening is seen as women's work. Illustrated in this study is the way in which changing gender relations can shape, as well as be shaped by, patterns of environmental change. It also argues that, for the Kuranko, the establishment of forest patches is a central part of land management, in contradiction to other studies which regard farming practices as causing deforestation.

165 **Agriculture in Guinea (Conakry).**
Bernhard Nett. In: *Agricultural transformation and social change in Africa.* Edited by Bernhard Nett, Volker Wulf, Abdramane Diarra. Frankfurt am Main, Germany: Peter Lang, 1992, p. 51-78. bibliog.

A general introduction to Guinea's geography is followed by historical background information on Guinea's development since pre-colonial times, and consideration of the impact of various policies on the current depressed state of 'traditional agriculture' in Guinea. It is argued that this key sector of the economy must be developed with policies sensitive to the people whose survival depends on it.

166 **The Popular Revolutionary Republic of Guinea: effective discrimination against small farmers in a socialist economy.**
Roger Shotton. In: *Poverty and rural development: planners, peasants and poverty.* Edited by K. Puttaswamaiah. New Delhi: Oxford & IBH Publishing Co., 1989, p. 380-98.

This is one of a collection of papers presented at a seminar held at the Institute of Development Studies (IDS), Brighton, in 1983. It was, therefore, written during Sekou Touré's period in government, and describes the deleterious effects on agriculture of the government's policies. During the early 1980s agricultural production stagnated due to the price structure and marketing system, and the management of the exchange rate, all of which were unfavourable towards small farmers.

L'avenir de la Guinée française. (The future of French Guinea.)
See item no. 54.

Guinea's economic performance under structural adjustment: importance of mining and agriculture.
See item no. 139.

Spécial Guinée. (Guinea special.)
See item no. 150.

Le foncier en Guinée. (Land tenure in Guinea.)
See item no. 168.

Salvage anthropology: the redesign of a rural development project in Guinea.
See item no. 169.

Assessing deforestation in the Guinea Highlands of West Africa using remote sensing.
See item no. 180.

Whose social forestry and why? People, trees and managed continuity in Guinea's forest-savanna mosaic.
See item no. 182.

Rural Development

167 **Tenure opportunities and constraints in Guinea: resource management projects and policy dialogue.**
Julie E. Fischer. *Land Tenure Center Newsletter, University of Wisconsin-Madison*, no. 72 (Winter 1994/95), p. 1-7.
With the beginning of the Second Republic in 1984, state landownership was abolished and the land was returned to customary landowners. This has led to many disputes over rightful ownership, particularly in the Fouta Djallon. The Land Tenure Center has undertaken projects in Guinea concerning land-tenure policy research, and aims to assist the Government of Guinea in drafting legislation to implement the national land code.

168 **Le foncier en Guinée.** (Land tenure in Guinea.)
Mondes en Developpement, vol. 21, no. 81 (1993), p. 1-95.
The entire issue of this journal is devoted to ten articles concerning land tenure in Guinea. Land tenure is a complex issue in Guinea, where many of the traditional agrarian rites are closely bound up with religion. Sekou Touré's First Republic nationalized land ownership, but under the Second Republic the land has gone back to private ownership. However, this has led to many disputes, which the government is attempting to settle with the introduction of legislation. These papers have abstracts in English, French and Spanish, and cover a variety of related issues. The papers are: 'Fondements philosophiques des rites agraires en Guinée' (Philosophical structures of agrarian rites in Guinea) by Boubacar Diakité; 'Les problèmes fonciers selon l'Islam' (Land tenure problems according to Islam) by Kélétigui Keita; 'Structures agraires et problèmes fonciers dans la communauté rurale de Koba-Tatéma (Boffa)' (Agrarian structures and land tenure problems in the rural community of Koba-Tatema) by Fodé Bangoura; 'Etude comparative des régimes fonciers en droits coutumiers Peul et Soussou' (Comparative study of the customary land tenure systems in Fula and Soussou regions) by Alseny Bah; 'Compromis entre régimes fonciers traditionnelles et modernes au centre urbain de Labé' (Compromise between traditional and modern land tenure systems in the urban centre of Labé) by Mamadou Dian Gongoré Diallo; 'Les systèmes fonciers traditionnels en Haute-Guinée: leur signification économique et sociale' (Traditional land tenure systems in Upper Guinea: their economic and

social significance) by Moussa Oularé and Lancei Kouyaté; 'Notion de propriété et conflits domaniaux en Guinée Forestiére: cas du pays Kissi' (Notion of ownership and property rights conflicts in the Forest Zone of Guinea: the case of the Kissi area) by Aly Gilbert Iffono; 'Impact de l'exploitation minière sur les régimes fonciers dans la région des monts Nimba' (The impact of mining on the land tenure systems in the Nimba Mountains region) by Julien Gbère Touré; 'Le droit foncier Guinéen' (The Guinean land tenure system) by Lamine Sidimé; and 'Verrouillage du système foncier rural: Département de Matam, rive gauche du fleuve Sénégal' (Locking up the rural land tenure system: Matam region, left bank of the Senegal River) by Madiodio Niasse.

169   **Salvage anthropology: the redesign of a rural development project in Guinea.**
Robert M. Hecht.   In: *Anthropology and rural development in West Africa*.   Edited by Michael M. Horowitz, Thomas M. Painter.
Boulder, Colorado: Westview, 1986, p. 13-26.

This chapter examines the redesign of the Guinea Agricultural Production Capacity and Development Project, a major scheme financed by the United States Agency for International Development, which was originally designed in 1975. By 1981 the project was foundering, but a salvage team was appointed in order to improve the project's effectiveness. The team included an anthropologist who gathered information on the social and economic features of the local Malinké peasants in order to include them in the scheme.

170   **Micro-projects in integrated local development: a popular response to post-socialism and structural adjustment in Guinea?**
Joseph Mullen.   *Journal of International Development*, vol. 1, no. 4 (1989), p. 487-95.

After a long period of central planning and structural adjustment programmes in the mid-1980s, it became apparent that large-scale development projects were failing to benefit the rural masses. Consequently there was a move towards small-scale integrated rural development projects which aim to involve the rural people themselves.

171   **L'Opération Konkouré-Boké: opération de coopération scientifique et technique.** (Operation Konkouré-Boké: scientific and technical cooperation.)
Office de la Recherche Scientifique et Technique Outre-Mer (ORSTOM).   Paris: ORSTOM, 1959. 51p. map. (Cahiers de l'ORSTOM, no. 2).

A study of the area likely to be affected by a proposed dam, which was planned to encourage the industrialization of the Konkouré area in Moyenne Guinée. It presents data on the geography, demography, ethnology, economy and agriculture of the area, and investigates the possible problems of the resettlement of people living in the area.

172　**Local programmes and national policies: NGO-state conflicts in Guinean rural development.**
Gerard Peart.　*European Journal of Development Research*, vol. 7, no. 1 (1995), p. 148-75. bibliog.
Examines the role of two NGOs (non-governmental organizations) in rural development schemes aimed at increasing smallholder production and productivity, in Wonkifong in Maritime Guinea. The paper assesses whether the NGOs' strategy undermined or failed to support national policies in the five sub-sectors of credit, fertilizers, seeds, water management infrastructure and marketing. It finds that, although the development schemes have been successful in raising smallholder productivity, the structural adjustment policies mean there is no market for the products.

Employment and Labour

173 **Guinée: pour une nouvelle syndicalisme en Afrique.** (Guinea:
      towards a new trade unionism in Africa.)
      Mid Diallo, Maurice Dopavogui, Gerard Kester.   Paris: L'Harmattan;
      Programme Africain pour le Développement de la Participation des
      Travailleurs (PADEP), 1992. 158p.

In 1986 the Programme Africain pour le Développement de la Participation des
Travailleurs set up a project for research and education aimed at securing the participation of Guinean workers in the country's development. This book examines the
conditions of workers and proposes the setting-up of trade unions in order to improve
working conditions.

174 **Pauvreté et marché du travail à Conakry (République du Guinée).**
      (Poverty and the labour market in Conakry.)
      Youssouf Dioubaté.   Geneva: Institut International d'Etudes Sociales,
      1992. 91p. bibliog. (Discussion Papers, no. DP/49/1992).

Presents the results of research on the relationship between poverty and the labour
market in Conakry. There are sections on: the structure and characteristics of
households; the structure of, and stratifications within, the labour market; and analysis
of the relationship between poverty and the labour market. The data collected appears
in a number of tables.

175 **Etude monographique sur l'emploi et la formation en Guinée.**
      (Study of employment and training in Guinea.)
      Ibrahima Guirassi.   [s.l.]: Centre Interafricain pour le Développement
      de la Formation Professionnelle, [1985]. 24+[21]p.

Reports on a mission to study the relationships between education, training and
employment in Guinea. The account includes surveys of Guinea's natural resources
and the system of professional training.

Statistics

176 **Bulletin Trimestriel d'Etudes et de Statistiques.** (Quarterly Bulletin of Statistics.)
Conakry: Banque Centrale de la République de Guinée, 1986- . quarterly.

Reports on the economic situation and presents financial figures on, for example, production, imports and exports.

177 **Bulletin statistique: numéro spécial.** (Statistical bulletin: special edition.)
Ministère du Plan et de la Coopération Internationale, Direction Nationale de la Statistique et d'Informatique. [Conakry]: Ministère du Plan et de la Coopération Internationale, 1990. 79p.

A set of tables divided into thirteen sections covering subjects such as: climate, population, employment, agriculture, manufacturing, mining, trade, price indices, transport, health and tourism.

Recensement général de la population et de l'habitat, fevrier 1983: analyse des résultats définitifs. (General census of population and living conditions, February 1983: analysis of final results.)
See item no. 93.

Environment and
Conservation

178 **L'originalité des mangroves de Guinée dans le monde tropical
humide.** (The uniqueness of the mangroves of Guinea in the humid
tropics.)
Frédéric Bertrand. *Les Cahiers d'Outre Mer*, vol. 44, no. 176 (1991),
p. 365-78. map. bibliog.

The Guinean mangrove swamps have unique features compared with other coastlines
of the humid tropics. This is due to a combination of the land environment, which is
favourable for the development of muddy zones, and a morphological-climatic
instability amplified by the degradation of the pre-forest savannas of the inland Fouta
Djallon region.

179 **Contested forests: modern conservation and historical land use in
Guinea's Ziama Reserve.**
James Fairhead, Melissa Leach. *African Affairs*, vol. 93, no. 373
(Oct. 1994), p. 481-512.

The Ziama forest in south-eastern Guinea is regarded as a relic of the diminishing
Upper Guinean forest formation. It was designated a forest reserve in 1932, made a
Biosphere reserve in 1981, and is now the subject of a major internationally-funded
conservation project. This paper looks at the history of the forest, beginning with
descriptions by 19th-century explorers who found the area heavily farmed and covered
by fields, fallow bush and grassland. Depopulation of the area was caused by late-
19th-century warfare and it was after this that the area reverted to forest. There is
currently antagonism from the local population towards the reserve, as they feel they
have historical rights to this land over which they have lost control.

180 **Assessing deforestation in the Guinea Highlands of West Africa using remote sensing.**
Peter T. Gilruth, Charles F. Hutchinson, Bademba Barry. *Photogrammetric Engineering and Remote Sensing*, vol. 56, no. 10 (1990), p. 1,375-82.

Assesses deforestation in an area of the Fouta Djallon by using historical and recent aerial mapping photography, large-scale video imagery and Landsat satellite imagery, to compare the amounts of agricultural clearance over thirty-five years. The results show a 48 per cent increase in permanent agriculture and a 526 per cent increase in shifting agriculture. This is partly due to a shortening of the fallow period in shifting cultivation, but also to an increase in the total agricultural area, which has expanded at the expense of the natural vegetation and has led to an increase in erosion.

181 **Natural resource management: the reproduction and use of environmental misinformation in Guinea's forest savanna transition zone.**
Melissa Leach, James Fairhead. *IDS Bulletin*, vol. 25, no. 2 (1994), p. 81-87.

This article examines the myth that the forest 'islands' in Guinea's Kissidougou prefecture are remnants of extensive forest cover; in fact, evidence shows that these areas of forest have been created by the local village inhabitants in an area of natural savanna. The authors explore how these inaccurate assessments are generated and validated by the various environmental policy institutions.

182 **Whose social forestry and why? People, trees and managed continuity in Guinea's forest-savanna mosaic.**
Melissa Leach, James Fairhead. *Zeitschrift für Wirtschaftsgeographie*, vol. 37, no. 2 (1993), p. 86-101.

This article looks at the relationship between the Kissi and Kuranko inhabitants of the Kissidougou area and the plants with which they live. It examines their environmental management and the ways in which their use of trees is integrated with agricultural production. It contradicts the assumptions by development workers that the local people are causing degradation of the forests.

183 **Politique forestière et plan d'action: principes et strategie.**
(Political forestry and action plan: principles and strategy.)
[Conakry]: Plan d'Action Forestier Tropical, 1988. various paginations. bibliog.

This is a development plan for forestry in Guinea with a strategy for the next twenty-five years, and an action plan for the period 1988-93. It also includes an extensive bibliography.

184 **Evolution politique, démographie et dynamique de
l'environnement en Guinée forestière.** (The political, demographic
and dynamic evolution of the environment in Forest Guinea.)
Georges Rossi. *Les Cahiers d'Outre-Mer*, vol. 46, no. 183 (1993),
p. 253-72.

The Lola region highlights the reaction of peasants to the various policies imposed
since independence, and illustrates the resulting consequences for the environment.
Under Sekou Touré production collapsed, and mass emigration of the local population
led to a serious agricultural crisis and the extension of the forest. However, since 1984
and the more liberal policies of the Second Republic, there has been a massive return
of the people, which, in turn, has caused demographic pressure, and is now resulting
in severe degradation of resources and disturbance of the ecological balance.

185 **Guinée: stratégie pour l'énergie domestique.** (Guinea: domestic
energy strategy.)
World Bank, Energy Sector Management Assistance Programme.
Washington, DC: World Bank, 1994. 77p. (Rapport, no. 163/94).

Fuelwood constitutes the principal source of energy in Guinea, and it is estimated that
demand will soon outstrip the natural production. This report examines the domestic
energy situation and related government policy, and suggests alternative energy
sources.

Education

186 Education and productive work in Guinea.

Amara Fofana. *Prospects: Quarterly Review of Education*, vol. 12, no. 4 (1982), p. 477-83.

Outlines the educational system under Sekou Touré's régime. New curricula were introduced in 1959 which were intended to place greater emphasis on the realities and problems of everyday life, rather than representing mere instruction. At the time that this paper was written, Guinea was in the second of three stages of 'school within daily life', in which schools were transformed into revolutionary education centres (CERs), and ethnic languages were used as the medium of instruction. Productive work was seen as the cornerstone between school and life. Since the end of Sekou Touré's government, education has returned to a more traditional school approach with French as the main medium of instruction.

187 La qualité de l'école primaire en Guinée: une étude de cas. (The quality of primary education in Guinea: a case study.)

Jean Yves Martin, Ta Ngoc Châu. Paris: Institut International de Planification de l'Education, 1993. 294p. bibliog.

A detailed report on a study, undertaken with the collaboration of the Guinean Ministry of Education, of primary education in six contrasting localities. At the time of the survey, in 1987-88, only twenty-eight per cent of school-age children were at primary school, and the research was carried out in order to identify factors that could enable the level of education to be raised.

Women literacy in Guinea.

See item no. 118.

Etude monographique sur l'emploi et la formation en Guinée. (Study of employment and training in Guinea.)

See item no. 175.

Literature

Novels

188 La source d'ébène. (The origin of ebony.)
Kiri Di Bangoura. Paris: L'Harmattan, 1991. 128p.
A novel contrasting the horrors of prison camp with the joys of village life.

189 Tropical circle.
Alioum Fantouré, adapted into English by Dorothy S. Blair. Harlow,
England: Longman, 1981. 259p.
Translated from the French, *Le cercle des tropiques* (Présence Africaine, 1972), this is
a novel about a fictional French colony based on Guinea, which describes the power
struggles leading up to independence, and the emergence of a tyrannical leader.

190 The African child.
Camara Laye, translated by James Kirkup, introduction by William
Plomer. London: Fontana, 1959. 159p.
Camara Laye was Guinea's best-known writer. This is an autobiographical novel
based on the author's childhood in Guinea that includes accounts of the traditions and
ceremonies of the Malinké community in which he was brought up, before he left to
study in Paris. It describes his discoveries of the world around him and his feelings for
his friends and family. The book was greeted with great critical acclaim when it was
first published. It is a translation of *L'enfant noir* (Paris: Plon, 1953), and was first
published in English as *The dark child* (London: Collins, 1955).

191 A dream of Africa.
Camara Laye, translated from French by James Kirkup. London:
Collins, 1968. 191p.
This tells the story of Fatoman, a character based on Camara Laye himself and his
own experiences, who tries to blend two cultures – French and traditional Malinké –

67

and comes to realize that neither culture has a place in his native land after its independence. It presents a portrait of Guinea and the effects of a changing political system. The book is a translation of *Dramouss* (Paris: Plon, 1966).

192 **The guardian of the word.**
 Camara Laye, translated from French by James Kirkup.   London: Fontana, 1980. 223p.

Originally published as *Le maître de la parole* (Paris: Plon, 1978), this novel tells of the ancient kingdom of Mali and its powerful leader, Mari Diata. It is a story that has survived in Malinké folktales to this day. This was the last novel of Laye, who died in 1980 in exile in Senegal.

193 **The radiance of the king.**
 Camara Laye, translated from French by James Kirkup.   London: Fontana, 1965. 284p.

This translation of *Le regard du roi* (Paris: Plon, 1954) is a novel which follows the travels of a white man, Clarence, through Africa on his quest for the King, symbolizing man's search for peace. The book is often compared with the works of Kafka.

194 **The bush toads.**
 Tierno Monénembo, translated from French by James Kirkup.
 Harlow, England: Longman, 1983. 136p.

This first novel by a Guinean in exile paints a picture of a country in turmoil, with society dominated by powerful and ruthless men. It is a translation of *Les crapauds-brousse* (Paris: Editions du Seuil, 1979).

195 **Un week-end à Conakry.** (A weekend in Conakry.)
 Jean Seignard.   Paris: L'Harmattan, 1990. 181p.

A novel set in 1970, during the attempted overthrow of Sekou Touré by the Portuguese. Seignard recounts the experiences of a sailor caught up with Portuguese commandos attempting to recapture their compatriots who were being held prisoner.

Criticism

196 **L'imaginaire dans les romans de Camara Laye.** (The imaginary in the novels of Camara Laye.)
 Ada Uzoamaka Azodo.   New York: Peter Lang, 1993. 165p. bibliog. (Studies in African and African-American Culture, no. 4).

This work examines the symbolism of Camara Laye's literature and includes a very extensive bibliography of writings about the author and his work.

197   **Camara Laye: a bio-bibliography.**
       Paul R. Bernard. *Africana Journal*, vol. 9, no. 4 (1978), p. 307-21.
       bibliog.

Six pages of biography are followed by the bibliography, which is divided into: works by Laye; material by him in periodicals; critical works on his literature; and compositions by Laye in anthologies.

198   **The writings of Camara Laye.**
       Adele King. London: Heinemann, 1980. 132p. bibliog. (Studies in African Literature).

A most informative book about Camara Laye and his work. Camara Laye, the best-known Guinean writer, was born in 1928 in Kouroussa, in Upper Guinea. After completing his schooling in Conakry, he won a scholarship to study engineering in Paris. His loneliness there prompted him to write of his childhood memories, which were published as *L'enfant noir* (Paris: Plon, 1953) and translated as *The African child* (q.v.). *Le regard du* roi (Paris: Plon, 1954) was translated as *The radiance of the king* (q.v.). By the time Laye returned to Guinea in 1956 he was well-known as an author and was a figure of some importance. After independence in 1958 he became ambassador to Ghana, where he continued writing. Due to his political activities he left Guinea in 1965. Like many other intellectuals who initially supported Sekou Touré at independence, Laye soon became critical and turned to the opposition when it became apparent that Touré was becoming a tyrannical dictator. It was in exile in Senegal that Camara Laye wrote his final book, *Le maître de la parole* (Paris: Plon, 1978), translated as *The guardian of the word* (q.v.). Laye died in Dakar in 1980.

199   **Littérature guinéenne.** (Guinean literature.)
       Notre Librairie, no. 88/89 (July-Sept. 1987), p. 1-203. bibliog.

The entire issue of this periodical is devoted to aspects of Guinean literature. A section on the cultural heritage includes articles on oral literature, Fula poetry and Arab-Islamic literature. Other features are: an article on Camara Laye, the best-known Guinean writer; a section on the country under Sekou Touré, who produced vast amounts of writing himself; some articles on the diaspora; and a section on present-day authors. Black-and-white photographs illustrate the text throughout.

200   **Special issue on Camara Laye.**
       Ngam: Occasional Papers of the Department of African Literature, University of Yaounde, Cameroon, no. 6 (1981). 122p.

A collection of eight articles on Camara Laye, with an editorial by Bernard Fonlon. The papers are: 'Self-identification and assimilation in *The dark child*' by Julien J. Lafontant (p. 5-13); 'Aliénation, conflit et authenticité dans *L'enfant noir* de Camara Laye' (Alienation, conflict and authenticity in Camara Laye's *L'enfant noir*), by Peter Igbonekwu Okeh (p. 14-31); '*Le regard du roi*: une pédagogie de la rédemption' (*Le regard du roi*: the teaching of redemption), by Grace Elonde-Ekoto (p. 32-55); 'Levels of thematic interpretation of Camara Laye's *Le regard du roi*' by Emil A. Magel (p. 56-72); 'Die Wahreit des "Den-Anderen-Sechens". Imagologische Untersuchungen zu Camara Laye: *Le regard du roi*' (The truth of 'the-other-ploughshare'. Research on imagery in Camara Laye: *Le regard du roi*), by Susanne Schroeder (p. 73-85); 'Camara Laye et la tentation de l'occident' (Camara Laye and the temptation of the west), by Gobina Moukoko (p. 86-107); 'Promenade avec Camara Laye dans le temple africain' (A walk with Camara Laye in the African temple), by Regine Donner (p. 108-18); and 'Etat présent de la recherche sur l'oeuvre de Camara Laye' (Current state of research on Camara Laye's work), by I. C. Tcheho (p. 119-22).

Poetry and folktales

201 **Clairière dans le ciel.** (Clearing in the sky.)
Sikhé Camara. Paris: Présence Africaine, 1973. 91p.

Like the writer's earlier collection of poems: *Poèmes de combat et de vérité* (Poems of struggle and truth) (Paris: Pierre Jean Oswald, 1967), this volume celebrates the glorious struggle for democratic revolution.

202 **Les nymphes du Sankarani.** (The nymphs of Sankarani.)
Mamadou Djan Pounthioum Diallo. Dakar: Khoudia Editions, 1989. 53p.

A collection of poems by a Guinean writer.

203 **Contes et récits peuls du Fouta Djalon.** (Fula stories and narratives from the Fouta Djallon.)
Collected by Bernard Salvaing, Korka Bah, Boubakar Bah. Paris: Conseil International de la Langue Française, 1985. 179p.

Collected in this volume are folktales, anecdotes, oral histories and fables, in Fula with French translations. There are several line illustrations.

204 **La femme, la vache, la foi: écrivains et poètes du Foûta Djalon.** (The woman, the cow, the faith: writers and poets of the Fouta Djallon.)
Edited by Alfâ Ibrâhîm Sow. Paris: Julliard, 1966. 375p. (Classiques Africains, no. 5).

A collection of poetry in Fula (Peul) with French translations. There is a Fula-French lexicon included at the back of the book. The poems, which were collected in the Fouta Djallon, are divided into two sections: formalized aristocratic literature and popular literature based on traditional styles and folklore.

205 **Poèmes peuls du Fouta Djallon.** (Fula poems from the Fouta Djallon.)
Gilbert Viellard. *Bulletin de Comité d'Etudes Historiques et Scientifiques de l'Afrique Occidentale Française*, (1934), p. 225-311.

This article presents a collection of eight poems in Fula, with French translations. They are divided into two sections: the first four are satirical poems about the situation in Guinea under French colonialism; the second four are about women.

Culture and the Arts

206 **Cultural policy in the Revolutionary People's Republic of Guinea.**
Paris: UNESCO, 1979. 90p.
Examines the effects of Sekou Touré's socialist cultural revolution on the country's cultural life. There are chapters on education, languages, scientific research, culture and the arts. It represents a rather bland and non-critical overview.

207 **Festival National des Arts et de la Culture.** (National Festival of
Arts and Culture.)
Conakry: Imprimerie Nationale, 1982. 2nd ed. 222p. (Révolution
Démocratique Africaine, no. 149).
This is an account of the twelfth National Festival which was held in November 1979. The events covered disciplines including theatre, literature, cinema, sculpture and sport. There are a number of photographs throughout the text, and texts of the inevitable addresses by Sekou Touré.

Music

208   **Guinée: recits et epopées (Guinea: narratives and epics). Record review.**
Roderic C. Knight. *Ethnomusicology*, vol. 38, no. 3 (1994), p. 552-57.
A review of a CD recorded by Patrick Larue (Ocora C560009, 1992), which presents fifteen examples of Fula, Guerzé, Toma and Malinké music played on traditional instruments. The CD has accompanying notes in French, with English and German translations.

209   **Musique Malinké: Guinée. Record review.**
Roderic C. Knight. *Ethnomusicology*, vol. 18, no. 2 (1974), p. 337-39.
Knight reviews a record of Malinké music recorded by G. Rouget (Vogue LDM 30 113, 1972, Collection Musée de l'Homme). One side of the record is devoted to *jali* or court music, and the other side contains village music. There is singing accompanied by the traditional instruments of kora, harps, lutes, percussion and drumming. The record is accompanied by comprehensive notes and photographs.

210   **Some revolutionary songs of Guinea.**
Djibril Tamsir Niana. *Présence Africaine, English Edition*, vol. 1, no. 29 (1960), p. 101-15.
A collection of a number of songs written at the time of independence, in Malinké and Soussou with English translations, which praise the revolution and Sekou Touré.

211 **Les Kissi: une société noire et ses instruments de musique.** (The
Kissi: a black society and their musical instruments.)
André Schaeffner. Paris: Hermann, 1951. 86p. (L'Homme: Cahiers
d'Ethnologie, de Géographie et de Linguistique, no. 2).

This is a detailed study of the music and musical instruments of the Kissi, who have a
large variety of drums and other percussion instruments as well as string and wind
instruments.

212 **Toward a Kpelle conceptualization of music performance.**
Ruth M. Stone. *Journal of American Folklore*, vol. 94, no. 372
(1981), p. 188-206.

Although this is a study of Guerzé (Kpelle) actually living in Liberia, the Guerzé, who
number about 340,000, also extend across the border into Guinea and this paper is also
relevant to them. It attempts to explore patterns of Guerzé conceptualization of music
performance. The Guerzé are particularly attuned to audio phenomena, with many
words in their vocabulary being imitations of the sound produced by the object
described. Several aspects of their music are quite different from Western music
concepts.

Libraries and Archives

213 Archival research in Guinea-Conakry.
David C. Conrad. *History in Africa*, vol. 20 (1993), p. 369-78.

In 1992 a new building was opened in Conakry for Les Archives Nationales du Guinée. This article reports on a visit to inspect and assess the archives, which include: government publications; colonial documents and collections of maps; photographs; and newspapers. The paper also lists some titles of 'Mémoires de diplôme' (dissertations) of students graduating from the University of Conakry. However, the Bibliothèque Nationale, in contrast, was said to be in a poor condition.

214 Report on archives of the Popular and Revolutionary Republic of Guinea in Conakry.
Martin A. Klein. *History in Africa*, vol. 8 (1981), p. 333-34.

Represents not much more than a note on the Guinea archives. Despite earlier reports to the contrary, the author found them generally in good condition and well-organized. He lists the various categories to be found.

Periodicals

215 **Études Guinéennes.** (Guinean Studies.)
   Conakry: Institut Français d'Afrique Noire, 1947-55. irregular.
This journal published scholarly articles on the geography, anthropology, history, customs and languages of Guinea. It is certainly worth referring to for articles which have not been listed separately in this bibliography. It was superseded by *Recherches Africaines* (q.v.).

216 **Horoya.**
   Conakry. weekly.
As the only newspaper to appear with any regularity, it carries local and African stories, but little international news. A number of other newspapers, mostly linked to political parties, have sprung up since the relaxing of attitudes towards political opposition.

217 **Jeune Afrique.** (Young Africa.)
   Paris: Le Groupe Jeune Afrique, 1960- . weekly.
A current affairs journal covering Francophone Africa, which often contains news items on Guinea.

218 **Recherches Africaines.** (African Research.)
   Conakry: Institut National de Recherches et de Documentation,
   1959-[1971]. quarterly.
This was originally published under the title *Études Guinéennes* (q.v.). It was a scholarly journal covering Guinean affairs, and included articles on history, geography and natural history, many by well-known writers and scholars. The majority of articles are on Guinea, but some are on West Africa generally. Individual articles are not included in this bibliography. There is no equivalent currently being published.

219 **West Africa.**
London: West Africa Publishing Co. Ltd., 1917- . weekly.

This weekly magazine is a major source for up-to-date information and news in English about Guinea.

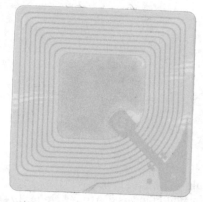

Bibliographies

220 **Guinée: mise au jour du patrimoine ou retour aux sources.**
(Guinea: updating of heritage or return to sources.)
Roger Botte. *Journal des Africanistes*, vol. 63, no. 1 (1993),
p. 93-138.

A bibliography of theses in human science presented at the University of Conakry
since 1968 and the University of Kankan since 1970. An analytical introductory
section is followed by a list of 777 theses with a subject index.

221 **Guinea, Ivory Coast, and Senegal: a bibliography on development.**
Lawrence Busch.   Monticello, Illinois: Council of Planning
Librarians, 1973. 48p. bibliog. (Exchange Bibliographies, no. 427).

Includes 320 items on Guinea, divided into books and pamphlets, articles, and
government publications. There is of course nothing up to date, but it is nonetheless
useful as it includes many items in English.

222 **Eléments de bibliographie concernant la Guinée.** (Elements of
bibliography concerning Guinea.)
Joanny Guillard.   Conakry: Ambassade de France, Mission Française
de Coopération et d'Action Culturelle, 1988. [unpaginated]. bibliog.

This bibliography includes 627 items arranged in one sequence alphabetically by
author or title. Particular attention is given to accounts of early voyages and travels in
Guinea and descriptions from the end of the 19th century. Virtually all references are
in French and include journal articles. There are thematic and chronological indexes.

223 **Bibliographie critique des sources imprimées de l'histoire de la Guinée publiées avant 1914.** (Annotated bibliography of printed sources on the history of Guinea published before 1914.)

Baba Ibrahima Kaké. Dakar: Université de Dakar, 1961. 72p. bibliog.

An annotated bibliography of historical works on Guinea, many by early travellers. Arranged in chronological order, the majority date from the end of the 19th century.

224 **Bibliographie sur la Guinée.** (Bibliography on Guinea.)

Organisation for Economic Cooperation and Development, Development Centre. Paris: OECD, 1965. 46p. bibliog.

This bibliography was compiled in connection with a seminar on Economic Development held in Guinea in 1965. It covers books, documents and articles on Guinea and its economic development, and is divided into sections by subject. Unfortunately it is now very out of date, but nevertheless it includes a wealth of references.

225 **Chronique de Guinée.** (Guinea chronicle.)

Jean Suret-Canale. *Cultures et Développement*, vol. 10, no. 2 (1978), p. 297-314; vol. 15, no. 4 (1983), p. 743-65.

Two articles which discuss writings about Guinea. The first, written during Sekou Touré's government, when it was not prudent to be critical of the régime, assesses various material written about the country, of which there was not much. The second article, although in a publication dated 1983, was actually written after Sekou Touré's death in 1984, when the situation was quite different. The article assesses a number of writings on the country, its political future and its economy.

Area handbook for Guinea.
See item no. 5.

Historical dictionary of Guinea (Republic of Guinea/Conakry).
See item no. 33.

Camara Laye: a bio-bibliography.
See item no. 197.

Index

The index is a single alphabetical sequence of authors (personal and corporate), titles of publications and subjects. Index entries refer both to the main items and to other works mentioned in the notes to each item. Title entries are in italics. Numeration refers to the items as numbered.

S

Sacred forest: the fetishist and magic rites of the Toma 97
Sahn, D. E. 137
Sainville, L. 78
Salimou, Al Hadj, Muslim teacher 113
Salvaing, B. 91, 203
Samori, une révolution dyula 42
Sanderval, A. O. Vicomte de 25-26
Sangaredi-Boké, bauxite mining 159
Sanneh, L. 112
Schaeffner, A. 211
Schroeder, S. 200
Schwartz, J. 149
SEEG *see* Société d'Exploitation des Eaux de Guinée
Seignard, J. 195
Sékou Touré 79
Sékou Touré: le héros et le tyran 88
Sekou Touré's Guinea: an experiment in nation building 57
Senegal
    Badiaranke 106
    bibliographies 221
    Guinea boundary 11
Senegal River, land tenure 168
Serfs, peasants, and socialists: a former serf village in the Republic of Guinea 96
Sexual behaviour, adolescents 114
Shotton, R. 166
Sidimé, L. 168
Sierra Leone
    Mano River Union 131
    Mende carvings 102
    trade 38
Sierra Leone studies at Birmingham 1988 49
Simon, D. 130
Skelton, Elizabeth Frazer, slave trader 40

Skurnik, W. A. E. 60
Slave trade 41, 56
    contracts 35
    end 39
    women 40
Slaves, emancipation 52
Slowe, P. M. 34, 130
Social indicators 147
Social organization 45
Social structure 115
    changes 116
Société d'Exploitation des Eaux de Guinée (SEEG) 123
Société Nationale des Eaux de Guinée (SONEG) 123
Society 5, 142
    colonial period 50
Socio-economic indicators, women 119
SONEG *see* Société Nationale des Eaux de Guinée
Souaré, O. 155
Soumah, A. M. 155
La source d'ébène 188
Soussou
    land tenure 168
    language 109
    music 210
    rituals 90
Sow, A. I. 204
Sow, D. 118
Stanley, Lord 27
Statistics 1, 176-77
Stevens, L. A. 19
Stone, R. M. 212
Stratégie de coopération de l'UNICEF dans le domaine de la santé publique en Guinée 121
Structural adjustment 139, 145-46, 151-52
    agriculture 162
    aluminium industry 158
    trade implications 153
Structure du badiaranke de Guinée et du Sénégal: phonologie, syntaxe 106

Sugiyama, Y. 31
Summers, A. 55
Suret-Canale, J. 7, 56, 80, 113, 225
Susu *see* Soussou
Sutherland, D.G. 20

T

Tableau de Bord de l'Economie Guinéenne 148
Tagliaferri, A. 102
Tcheho, I. C. 200
Telli, Diallo
    biographies 89
    Boiro prison camp 66
Third World regional development: a reappraisal 130
Thompson, V. 76
Thompson, W. 27
Timbo
    exploration 25, 27
    Hubbu movement 110
Toma
    music 208
    rituals 97
Topol, Y. 151
Touba, holy place 113
Toucouleurs, proverbs 108
Touré, Ahmed Sekou 34, 57-84
    agricultural policies 166
    assessment 71
    atrocities 63, 65
    authored works 81-82, 136
    biographies 79, 88
    chieftaincy end 69, 80
    cultural policy 206
    economic reconstruction 141
    ideology 57, 60, 81-82
    independence 51, 68-69, 72, 74
    international policy 136
    isolationism 128
    legal system 127
    national integration 128, 130
    1970 invasion 70

Map of Guinea

This map shows the more important towns and other features.

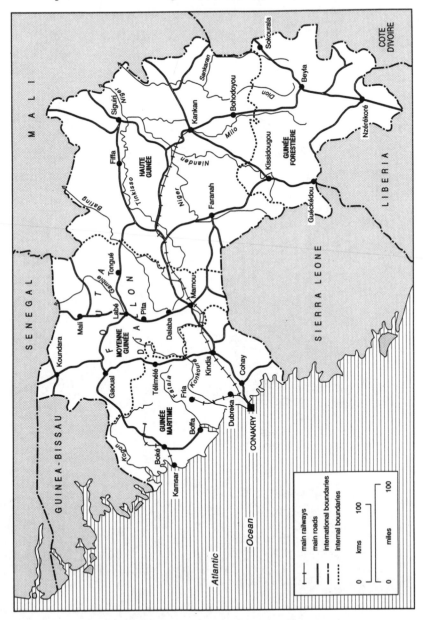

ALSO FROM CLIO PRESS

INTERNATIONAL ORGANIZATIONS SERIES

Each volume in the International Organizations Series is either devoted to one specific organization, or to a number of different organizations operating in a particular region, or engaged in a specific field of activity. The scope of the series is wide-ranging and includes intergovernmental organizations, international non-governmental organizations, and national bodies dealing with international issues. The series is aimed mainly at the English-speaker and each volume provides a selective, annotated, critical bibliography of the organization, or organizations, concerned. The bibliographies cover books, articles, pamphlets, directories, databases and theses and, wherever possible, attention is focused on material about the organizations rather than on the organizations' own publications. Notwithstanding this, the most important official publications, and guides to those publications, will be included. The views expressed in individual volumes, however, are not necessarily those of the publishers.

VOLUMES IN THE SERIES